Maggie's

1980-2020

Too Much Fun

MAGGIE'S

1980-2020

Too Much Fun

Sponsors: Katherine Hayes and Molly Rice
Proofing and Editing: Heidi Nelson, Terri Wagner, Margie Erickson, Ros Nelson, Becky Lind
Book Creation and Publisher: Ros Nelson at Little Big Bay LLC

ISBN: 978-0-9968071-8-0

Little Big Bay LLC
littlebigbayshop.com

1980-2020

Too Much Fun

Lake Superior's Own

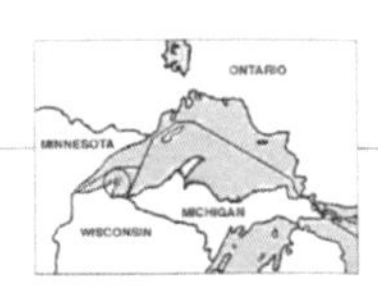

Breakfast with "the Queen of Bayfield"

"I didn't want to be a rich bitch. I did it with hard work."

ROSLYN NELSON

Ed Erickson, 85-years young and the subject of LSM's Heritage department in the June/July 1994 issue, joins Mary at the table in Maggies. The ever-enterprising Mary Rice has helped to document his memories and those of other senior members of Bayfield on videotape.

I can't be more wrong.
She comes in Maggies' side door right on time, sporting red, heart-

"It's been a lot of fun for me personally," she says.

How the Queen got her name

One of the streets in Bayfield, Wisconsin, is named for Henry M. Rice, a Minnesota territorial delegate and, later, U.S. senator. In years to come, however, it's possible that people seeing the Rice name on the street markers will think the street is named for Mary Rice.

For 10 years, I had heard admiring stories about her influence in the northern Wisconsin community. Who is Mary Rice, I wonder … this woman I have come to think of as the "Queen of Bayfield"?

I know that she is thought of as a benefact- and philanthropist, and in her own words, an eccentric. **I also know that she owns Maggie's, the restaurant on Manypenny Avenue** where we agreed to meet at 9 a.m. on a Sunday morning.

I picture her as a proper woman in her 60s: cardigan sweater, pearls and white hair.

I can't be more wrong.

She comes in Maggie's' side door right on time, sporting red heart-shaped glasses, a colorful dress and numerous rings. Her style is straightforward right from the start and by the time our two-hour breakfast is over, I have decided that this woman is one of few people with equal access to both sides of the brain; an entrepreneur with the soul of an artist.

The oldest child, Mary grew up anticipating an active role in Andersen Windows, the family business. That expectation unmet, her business instinct flowed into some of Bayfield's classic enterprises: the famous Bates Bar, Maggie's Restaurant, and The Clubhouse on Madeline Island. She is partner in other investments and has been in Bayfield long enough that some endeavors, like Main Street Maggie's, a breakfast and lunch restaurant, have come and gone.

"It's been a lot of fun for me personally," she says. "It was really interesting to be here and be doing things that are a part of the community and are also enjoyable."

Mary spent childhood summers on Sand Island in the Apostle Islands and winters in Bayport, Minnesota. She remembers the excitement of exploring sand caves and swimming in the cold water of Lake Superior.

Marriage to a medical student took her to Europe one year after graduation from Carlton College. Sixteen years later, divorced and with two daughters, she found herself back in St. Paul—with Bayfield summers a tradition once more.

Finally, in June 1980 she moved to Bayfield permanently. By then, she says, she had financial security. She originally planned to enjoy a year of relative peace and quiet—a retreat from the noise of the world—but, in a year she found herself starting Maggie's instead.

"I didn't want to be a rich bitch. I did it with hard work," she says, then starts to laugh. "I kept the wraps on until I came back—with a Mercedes. That sort of let my financial situation out of the bag!"

It seems impossible to believe that anyone could see Mary as anything but self-created. Maggie's, the restaurant where we sit, is a case in point. Pink flamingos are the ubiquitous motif. They are stuffed and hanging off the wall, or framed and tacked to the ceiling. They're everywhere!

"The flamingos started off as a joke in awfulness. The stuff just pours in the door. The train? Another screwy idea. (Ask the bartender and he turns on a model train that chugs around on a ledge near the ceiling.) "Another restaurant in Florida, the Bubble Room, had a train. We used to have a pool table right over there and we danced on it"

Our breakfast is interrupted frequently by relatives and friends. Everyone seems to know and like Mary and she likes them.

I ask about her family, the Hulings of Bayport, and how she gets along with her ex-husband.

"My parents lived in Bayport, Minnesota. My dad had Parkinson's disease for 20 years. He was tough."

"Are you like him?"

She roars. "Yes I am just as stubborn!"

Mary is equally enthusiastic about her ex-husband and his second wife. She says they had a 25th "non-anniversary," where he found himself posing with a wife on each side.

In the 1980s, when Mary was in her 40s, she saw herself as a far-sighted business woman. She sensed that tourism would be a bigger part of Bayfield's future and was only surprised that it took longer than she expected. Now, with her businesses well-established, her attention has turned to watercolor painting. Letting go of control over her businesses in order to develop herself as an artist was a challenging mid-life decision.

"I have two favorite sayings: Life is too short to be boring and I'm having way too much fun!"

She adores painting and studies with Karlyn Holman in nearby Washburn, whom she credits as being an exceptional teacher. The students have been on painting trips to Guatemala, Italy, Norway, Sweden and Russia. And, of course, they have the incomparable light and landscape of Bayfield and the Apostle Islands at their doorstep.

"I still work hard for Northland College. I'm on the board of directors and head of the development committee but painting is still my personal goal."

Summing up her attitude about business, art or perhaps just life, she says, "I have a real low tolerance for bureaucracy. It's better to just get things done!"

Bayfield has weathered the economic highs and lows of lumbering, fishing and quarrying. Now tourism dominates. Mary has identified the kind of people drawn to settle in this picturesque town, perched on the edge of Lake Superior. "Bayfield attracts people with frontier mentality—risk takers and people who want to smell the roses." She certainly fits her own description.

Mary usually spends between nine and 11 months in Bayfield each year. She lives in one of the grand Bayfield-style homes, which is impeccably maintained. It's the same one she began renovation on when she moved back to stay in 1980. Of course, now it has a pink flamingo mailbox.

Flair. That's what she has. I see her once more before I leave town the next day. A handful of her thick, blond hair is pulled up into a big, white clip. It is 7 a.m. and she is off on a walk. "What else would you think I got up so early for?" she asks as she whirls out the door—doubtlessly smelling roses along with way.

—Roslyn Nelson / Printed with kind permission from Lake Superior Magazine, Aug.-Sept. 1994

WANTED

CONSIDERED TO BE EXTREMELY DANGEROUS

COULD BE IN A BIRTHDAY PARTYING MOOD

MARY H. RICE

ALIAS: THE BOSS, BOSS MAGGS, MAGGIE, STELLA FEINSTEIN, BUTTS AND MAREBARE

THESE ARE JUST A FEW OF THE POSSIBILITIES,
DON'T BE FOOLED BY THE NAME!

KNOWN TO FREQUENT: THE BEACH HOUSE , THE DOCK AND THE BLUE ROOM AT SAND IS., TABLE 5 AT MAGGIES, HER WOMB, THE BOARD ROOM AT A.CORP., THE RITZ CARLTON--SHY TOWN,THE ST. PAUL HOTEL, ON REALLY HOT DAYS DRIVING AROUND IN HER AIR CONDITIONED MERCEDES OR WHERE EVER A GOOD TIME CAN BE HAD.

IF LOCATED: DO NOT ATTEMPT TO APPREHEND OR WISH HER A HAPPY BIRTHDAY, SHE CLAIMS TO HAVE FIGURED OUT A WAY TO STOP HAVING THEM. DON'T BE DUPED BY HER PERFECT DEMEANOR, THIS WOMAN IS CAPABLE OF ANYTHING!

liv-er-u
Maggie's
is 35 years...
but the livers are fresh
1980 - 2015

Maggie's
Bayfield, WI
Just Add
Flamingo's

The people make it happen

THE GIRLS

Molly and I saw "Maggie's become Maggie's." We brought friends and hung around while grown-ups cleaned and fixed things. **During the first years, we ate dinner there most nights.** Other constants were the jukebox and Ms. Packman. Cindy, the main cook, was a surrogate older-sister-mom to us.

As a teenager, I was plagued by the fact that my mom owned two bars and I would never be able to "get served" when underage. Crazy to think about that now when I have kids that age myself.

Once I no longer lived in Bayfield, a strange think started to happen. **I would go to Maggie's and not recognize the staff. It was slow at first, but as the years flew by it happened more often.** As a kid, I would bus my own dishes. When relationships with the staff became less familiar, I stopped doing it very often. One night, however, I entered the kitchen and saw Karmyn Hauser, who I hadn't seen in years. It practically brought tears to my eyes because we had lost contact. In early childhood our families picnicked at Sand Bay every summer Sunday. Finding her unexpectedly was a gift. I was able to meet her and other friends' children as they began to work at Maggie's, too.

In recent years, Maggie's became a second dining room again. Pretty much every time my kids and I visited we would go there, mostly with Mom at "her table." My children developed a craving for Maggie's. So many milestones have been celebrated there with Mom—from highchairs to eventually a kids' table while the grownups filled Mom's table. Sevy's (Sevona) favorite was grilled cheese. TJ's (Tysen) go-to was mac 'n' cheese; he went from one to two to be satisfied. My favorite was the fish livers. I will really miss them. I've tried to make them myself, but they never taste just right.

I'm especially sad that the pandemic resulted in the accelerated end to both Maggie's and my mom. But, it is somehow heartwarming that their paths ended together. It would have been hard to continue to dine there without Mom. And, it would have been hard to visit her without the comfort of Maggie's food. **Mom and Maggie's were inseparable from the very beginning. Unless she was out of town, I don't think there was more than a day or two that passed, in all the 40 years, that Mom did not eat at Maggie's. It was her office, kitchen, and dining room.**

Top: Daughters Katherine Hayes, Molly Rice, with Mary in the middle. Above, l-r: Katherine, Alison, Molly. Below, l-r: Alison, Molly, Katherine

People knew that's where they could find her. Maggie's couldn't live without Mary, and Mary couldn't live without Maggie's.

—*Katherine Hayes, Mary's second daughter*

Below: Barbara Rice, Alison's mother

Katherine, Molly

Requests

Beans, rice recipe sent by Maggies of Bayfield

The black beans and rice served at Maggies in Bayfield, Wis., are delicious. Would they share their recipe? Thank you.
Martha Larson, St. Paul

Janel Ryan of Maggies Restaurant, 257 Manypenny Av., Bayfield, Wis., sent this recipe and said you can serve salsa on the side if desired.

Maggies Restaurant Black Beans and Rice

2 c. black beans, soaked overnight
5 c. water
½ c. corn oil
½ large onion, peeled and halved
1 tbsp. salt
Rice:
¼ c. corn oil
½ large onion, finely diced
1 large garlic clove, diced
1½ c. rice
3 c. water
½ tbsp. salt
Sour cream, optional
Grated cheddar cheese, optional
Chopped green onions, optional

Bring the 5 cups of water and beans to a boil, lower temperature and simmer ½ hour. Add oil, onion and salt, bring to a boil again, reduce heat and simmer 1 more hour. Beans are done when they are soft but not mushy; the liquid should be thick. Take off heat and discard the onion.

For rice, sauté onion in oil over medium low heat for 5 minutes. Add garlic and continue to sauté until soft and golden brown. Strain mixture, reserving onion/garlic mix and return oil to the pan; add rice and sauté until golden, stirring continually for 10 minutes. Add reserved onion mix, water and salt to rice. Bring to a boil, reduce heat and cover. Simmer 10 minutes. Remove from heat and let stand 5 minutes with lid on to absorb remaining liquid.

Place cooked rice on plate, make a well in center and place cooked black beans in the well. Top with sour cream, cheddar cheese and green onions if desired. Makes 4 to 5 servings.

(1 serving or 1/5 recipe, without garnish = 1 vegetable exch., 4 bread/ starch exch., 6½ fat exch.; 601 calories, 68 gm. carbohydrate, 11 gm. protein, 33 gm. fat, 2640 mg. sodium, 0 mg. cholesterol and 93 mg. calcium.)

Mary, Molly, Katherine.

SECOND KITCHEN

Alison (Cody) Urhammer is John (in background) and Barbara Rice's daughter

My memories go back about 35 years. There are so many, but to sum it up, I was always excited to go to Maggie's when I visited Mary. I looked forward to being there with my family. It was a "second kitchen."

—*Alison Urhammer*

"The kids" ...

Above: Brianne Erickson and Buster Bean
Below, l-r: Brodi Anderson Erickson, Buster Bean, Tyler Lind

Above: Sean Erickson

Below: Mary's granddaughter Sevy Hayes

Above: Granddaughter Claire
Below: Granddaughter Claire and Mary

Above: Dan and son Sam Priebe

At right: Grandson Sam

Below: Brody Andersen Erickson, Margie Erickson, Brianne Erickson

Above, at left: Granddaughter Sevy (Sevona) Hayes
Below, l-r: Grandson TJ (Tyson), Drew Barker

Heidi Nelson: there from the start

In the waning days of Maggie's and after Mary's passing, I could only look back and remember how fortunate I was to be there in the beginning. Despite the great sadness of losing both, looking back on the first days of Maggie's would make me smile. It's hard to believe that 40 years ago Mary

Connie J Marcy's clock from Juniors Bar "still works." Juniors, 1966-77, was owned by Junior Yeska. Fishermans Cove 1978-80 was owned by Bob and Donna Bissell. Mary purchased it from them in 1980.

walked into the **Rear Admiral** (now Sgt. Pepperoni's), a gift shop she opened in May of 1980 and where I was first employed and said, **"I bought a bar, you want to move over there?" Maggie's** was the first of many **"Hot damn, I've got an idea!"** schemes.

In the opening days and years, Mary was a larger than life presence in the little bar on the corner of Manypenny and Third. She developed both the food and bar menus, wrote the recipes, trained the staff, cooked on the line, scrubbed dishes, bartended, served, hosted, danced on the pool table, and entertained all who came in. After the first year, there was no doubt that Mary had planted the seed for what was to become the first of many food ventures in the town that had won over her heart during her childhood years.

Maggie's

NICKNAME

At my father's funeral, Mary told us that our dad, John Hauser, gave Maggie's its name. It was his nickname for her. —*Barb Schullo*

In 1981, Mary's Hot Damn Idea! was if one **Maggie's** was good, two would be better, hence **Main Street Maggie's** was born. Purchasing the former Goldman's Cafe from Pauline and Lloyd Goldman gave Mary a breakfast restaurant and an "uptown presence." After two years, she closed Main Street Maggie's and along with Randy Anderson, who had been working there, expanded her footprint to Madeline Island. After hiring Jim Webster, formerly of Schiek's in Minneapolis, to be the chef and with Randy managing the front of the house, Mary had her white tablecloth restaurant: **The Clubhouse**

on Madeline Island. It closed in 1999 when Mary made plans to build her final venture, **Wild Rice Restaurant** which opened in August of 2001 led by the same team of Jim and Randy.

In between the first and last restaurant, Mary diversified her portfolio by adding **Bates Bar**, which provided a summer music schedule that kept Ronnie and Billy Boutin taking turns coming to the back door yelling, "turn down the damn music!" I guess getting up at 4 a.m. to get on the lake justified their request!

The **Cheeseboard**, purchased from Guy and Kathie Habeck, was a summer-only shop that provided takeout sandwiches and a diverse selection of great cheeses and deli products.

With **Morty's Pub**, the iconic Bayfield bar of Morty Baldwin and Greg and Gail Kinney, Mary continued the tradition of, "Purveying the Pinnacle in Potent Potables." Its history on Rittenhouse Avenue deserves its own book!

Janel Ryan and Debbie Lind were the ladies of **Two Girls Catering** at Bates Bar. Janel had been the chef and kitchen manager at Maggie's and brought her creativity and expertise to this catering operation.

The **Egg Toss Bakery Café** brought Mary back into the breakfast business in 1996. Thousands of Fishermans Platters were devoured and her development of the Eggs Benedict menu became an instant classic with the Crabby Benny leading the charge. One day when the Hollandaise sauce wasn't up

to her standards, into the kitchen she went and gave an immediate tutorial to the staff on how to make it from that point on.

In 2001 **Wild Rice Restaurant** was her final gift of culinary genius to the Chequamegon Bay region. For 16 years, the creative staff reveled in Mary's original dreams of executing the finest food, drinks, and atmosphere for everyone to enjoy. For 40 years, we had it all in our own backyard and for that I say, **"Hot damn! Mary, you were the best and will never be forgotten!"**

Top: Julian Nelson's 100th birthday at Egg Toss. L-r: Clifford Hadland, Ron Boutin, Jimmy Erickson, Julian Nelson
At left: Julian Nelson

THE LONGEST EMPLOYEE

Starting the first day I worked, I waitressed, bartended, washed floors, counted money, did payroll, paid purveyors, ordered the booze, assisted with hiring, and hand-wrote the menus, until Mary figured out what she wanted on a printed menu! I refused to learn how to work the line because, in my own words, "I WOULD BE TERRIBLE AT IT and knew I'd never ever be able to get two hamburgers, a fish sandwich and whitefish livers put out all at the same time!" After my daughter Hayley was born in 1986, I bowed out of waitressing and bartending but still did all the office work for Maggie's and all of Mary's other businesses. "I'm still doing the last of the bill paying, while being retired, until the business and/or building is sold."

—*Heidi Nelson*

Final dinner at Wild Rice. L-r: Jim Webster, Mary Rice, Randy Anderson, John Rice

1991: Kris Connell, Heidi Nelson, Gary Holman at Mary's house for 1991 Northern New Year

Note: Rear Admiral, Inc. was the first corporation that Maggie's was organized under. Main St. Maggie's, Cheeseboard, Bates, and the Egg Toss fell under that corporation when they were purchased. Morty's was under Rittenhouse, Inc. and The Clubhouse was under Clubhouse, Inc. Mary was also a partner with the ski hill, Apostle Island Ski Corp, Inc., and Mt Ashwabay Bar, Inc. which she later ended up owning. In December, 1997 these corporations were rolled into one, initially Rear Admiral, Inc. and later, Flamingos Up North, Inc.. FUN's first directors' meeting was in 2000. Randy Anderson came up with the name because now there was more than one flipping flamingo! Wild Rice became a FUN, Inc. flock member in 2000. —Heidi Nelson

Mary Rice and Heidi at the Clubhouse in 1991

Maggie's: Early days, 1980s

NO ONE HAS EVER COME CLOSE

The burgers were the bomb at Juniors Bar. No one has ever come close. My grandmother said it was because of how his grill was seasoned.

—Sharon M. DeFoe Lewis

Maggie's: Early days, 1980s

Top left: "Mike Schultz used to dress as Elvis Presley and entertain us."

Above: Gerry Carlson. Salmo Construction, which Gerry owned, did the first remodel. Jim Smith was also a part of Salmo.

The people make it happen

OLYMPIC PAYROLL MEDAL

I started working for Mary Rice in October, 1986, working halftime on nutrition/lifestyle issues for Mary and with Heidi at Maggie's.

Back then, the Flamingos Up North (FUN) attic office at Maggie's (at right) was staffed by Heidi. "Old Bayfield style," it was complete with a small TV, mismatched furniture, and file cabinets. Back then the "soaps" ran back-to-back all day and Heidi had her favorites. I had never watched soaps but grew fascinated by the lack of progress shown by the characters and plots. I thought it pretty progressive that Mary was cool with having a TV in the office!

Anyone doing bookkeeping back then could relate to processing payroll with pencil and paper, looking up the "single" biweekly federal and state tax deduction—off the Government printed paper grid—each and every week for every single employee. We created a mountain of ledgers and calculator tape. Even worse were quarterly 941s, FUTA, WI unemployment filings, and typing multi-form W-2s.

Back then computers were new on the scene. I believe Heidi was using Sage software purchased by modules (Payroll/AR/AP or whatever the business needed). Sage was complicated, expensive, and we began to think—more than Maggie's needed.

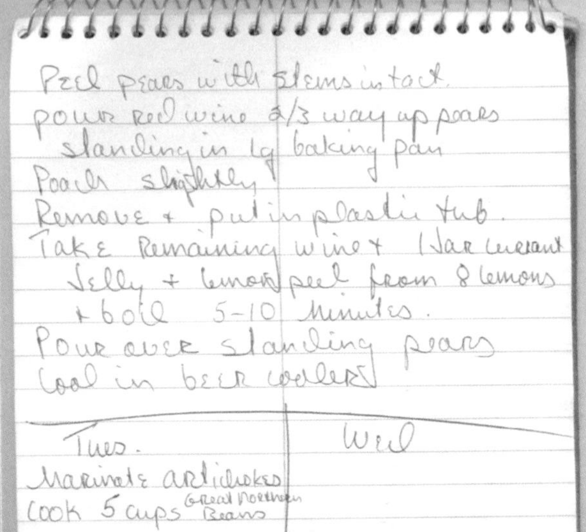

Peel pears with stems in tact.
pour red wine 2/3 way up pears
standing in lg baking pan
Poach slightly
Remove + put in plastic tub.
Take Remaining wine + Red currant
Jelly + lemon peel from 8 lemons
+ boil 5-10 minutes.
Pour over standing pears
Cool in beer coolers

Tues.
Marinate artichokes
Cook 5 cups Great Northern Beans

Wed

1995 Apple Festival. L-r: Deb Lind, Janel Ryan and Lois Stensvad, Steve Cvek, Kenny Dobson, Josh and Beth Degroot, Mike Skorcheski, Mary Kay Defoe

Duties and Responsibilites

COOKS

Prepare

Jams and jellies
compote
muffins
sausage/bacon
pancake batter
french toast batter
specials and or features
bagels
biscuits
soups
stock pot
salsa sauces
toppings for burgers
refried beans
sauerkraut
beer beef

PREPS

Prepare

potatoes-all varieties
fruit slices
slice bread
omelette fillers
pizza prep
sour cream and butter cups
slice cheeses-all varieties
ball 5 oz. burgers
italian salad
greek salad
pasta salad
clean lettuces
portion onion rings
sauces for wings
canadian bacon
ham, turkey, roast beef, corned beef
pepperoni
toppings for burgers
horseradish sauce
beer batter
bone fish
make salad dressings
clean berries
pizza orders
vegetables and toppings for salads

PIZZA LINE

	total	ON
all Pan on top Full to specifications		
Italian Sausage	1-1/6 Pan + 2 Bags	
Pepperoni	1-1/6 Pan + 2 Bags	
Canadian Bacon	1 Bag	
Chorizo Sausage	3 Bags	
diced Chicken	2 Bags	
Mozzarella cheese	2 containers	
Parmesan cheese	1-1/6 Pan + 1 Bag	
asiago cheese	1-1/6 Pan + 1 Bag	
Feta Cheese	1-1/6 Pan	
chopped onions	1-1/6 + 1 Bag	
chopped peppers	2 shallow 1/6 Pans	
chopped tomatoes	2-1/6 Pans	
Jalapenos	1-1/6 Pan + Backup	
sliced mushrooms	1-1/6 Pan + 1 Bag	
Black olives	2-1/6 Pans	
green olives	1-1/6 Pan Left in jar	
Kalamata olives	1-1/6 Pan + Left in jar	
artichoke hearts	2-1/6 Pans	
Pizza Doughs		
4 oz	25	
6 oz	25	
Spinach Leaves	4 qts	
roast peppers	1 shallow 1/6 Pan	
Pesto	2 1/6 Pans	

Viva la Mexico!

Thursday Dec. 12th

"Hola"

Experience our Southern neihbor on Mexican Night. A Mexican holiday dinner, fun and music at Maggies.

Menu

First Course – Broiled Shrimp with Carmelized garlic.

Second Course – Turkey breast Mole with Chorizo Sauss

Third Course – Traditional Flan with whip cream.

We will have limited Seating at 6:00 pm and 8:00 pm. So make your reservations early.

Price Per Person 16.95

#779-5641

I had recently set up Versa Professional (accounts receivable) and Peachtree (small business accounting software) at the Ferry Line. Practicing there made the installation easier for Heidi at Maggie's!

Heidi and I agreed to transition Maggie's from Sage to Peachtree complete accounting. Peachtree software was one price for the basic modules (GL/AP/AR/PR/P&L/balance sheets). It was simpler but no less terrifying that Heidi or I could make an entry and "screw it up." Peachtree back then was generational (one generation "closed" at the end of the month), unlike Quickbooks (perpetual) now. **Installing business software just for payroll felt like you had been awarded an Olympic medal or Nobel prize**. Nonetheless, whether PR was done by paper and pencil or with software, when everyone was enjoying Christmas and looking forward to New Year's, Heidi and I were losing sleep over the fact that the "4 part" W-2s wouldn't print right, line up, or if the totals matched the YTD totals.

Another tough lesson to learn was to be faithful in doing (labeling and storing off site) "floppy disk" accounting data backups. I remember doing a Peachtree backup taking upwards of six (or more) floppies. My mantra was, "do the darn backup or risk having to re-enter payrolls back to January first." Still another pothole was limited hard drive space. Storing Peachtree "generations" back to your start date filled up the hard drive. A user could be in the awkward position of the computer being unable to "load" an application (i.e. Peachtree) because the drive was full. The only option was to go in via DOS and start deleting files. You had better know what directory those data files were in and what the current "generation" was. Phew!

—Robin Trinko-Russell

I remember what it was like before I sold it, then, years later, being there for the first time. "Wow, they painted it in bright colors and changed some things!" Cool transformation and fabulous tenders! —Bob Bissell

---

The people make it happen

Above left: Gerry Cox, Richard Erickson. At right: Wayne Barningham, Vick Goodlet, Billy Arseneau. Below left: Brenda Erickson. Below right: "guys at the bar"

Above: Lulu Haskins, (child unknown), Margie Erickson and her sister Diane Barningham. Below: John Murphy, Mary Kay Defoe, Brenda Erickson

At left: Julie Zenner with Heidi Nelson

Julie Zenner, possibly from Channel 6, came to Maggie's with a video photographer and did a story on Maggie's.

Julie is now at Public Television WDSE.

Lenny Erickson and Bill Deragon

Upper left: Jim Webster and Heidi Nelson. Upper right: Phil Sunde aka Tiny, Margie Erickson, Morris Boutin
Above left: Mary Rice and Mark Jerabek. Above right: Hilda Reynolds and Chris Pederson

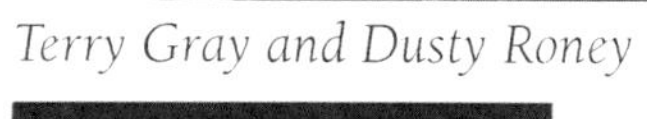

Terry Gray and Dusty Roney

Far left: John Hanson, Marian Goodlet

Left middle: Joyce Bratti

Left: Phil Sunde, Karmyn Simmons

The people make it happen

Above: Gina Karl, Mary Kay Defoe, Nancy Erickson
Below: Jimmy Erickson, Wayne Barningham, Vick Goodlet

Above: Mary at work in 1980. "I didn't want to be a rich bitch. I did it with hard work." Phil Peterson is in the background. Below: John Hauser, Karmyn Simmons

L-r: Jerry Gilbertson (Frog), Wayne Barningham

Bubsy Boutin

Maggie's Breakfast Club

Free Recession Insurance

Buy 9 Then Have One On Us

Name____________________

Privileges of Membership

VIP Treatment at Maggie's and a Six Month Paid Lease on One Square Foot of Maggie's Floor Space, Which You Can Stand on Any Time Maggie's is Open. Directions to Your Square Foot and Lease Maintenance Info. When You Sign.

Having fun in Bayfield

WHEN she moved to Bayfield on the shore of Lake Superior in 1980, **Mary Andersen-Rice** intended only to keep house and raise her two daughters. But her pipe dream was to own an inn. That led her to buy an old tavern near Bayfield's waterfront.

From that has come not only Maggie's, a trendy restaurant and bar, but also a group of popular entertainment spots in the area. She owns and manages two other Bayfield bars — Bates and Morties — and a cheese shop called the Cheeseboard; she's majority owner of the Mount Ashwabay Ski Resort; she operates the Big Top Chautauqua, a non-profit summer music theater; and, across the bay on Madeline Island, she has turned an old golf course clubhouse into the elegant Clubhouse Restaurant.

Next, she says, she wants to develop a $5 million inn on the harbor front.

Andersen-Rice, 48, a member of the family that owns the Andersen Window Corp. of Bayport, Minn., spent summers in Bayfield as a child. As an adult, she has become one of the city's leading entrepreneurs, philanthropists and promoters.

She has been a leading backer of such efforts as landscaping the library, saving an historic bridge from demolition and bringing a Catholic school building up to code.

"I feel I've grown into myself here in Bayfield," she says. And she's doing so with a grace and ease that underscores one of her typical remarks: "We're having way too much fun here."

—Mike Savage W

Mary Andersen-Rice: Behind food and fun in Bayfield

WHEN WE MET IN 1981

I first met Mary when I was in the Lost Nation String Band. We had moved up from Madison in 1980. Somehow we got booked for Mary's birthday party at Port Superior. One thing led to another and soon we found ourselves playing Bates Bar Sunday nights. That's when I really connected with Mary. Jump ahead to 1985. The Nelson-Ferris show, Riding The Wind, debuted in July 1985. Mary and her parents, Bill and Betty Hulings, attended the show, loved it, and wanted to build us a theatre. Wow! If it wasn't for them there would be no Big Top Chautauqua. They bought our first tent, a used big top, for around $2500. 1986 was our first season. The tent leaked in rains. Over the years their support increased. The last time I saw dear Mary was February, 2020 at the Harbor View Event Center in Washburn. I came over at intermission to give her a hug. She said "I needed to hear some live music." RIP Mary. No one has ever given more help to me than Mary Rice.

—*Warren Nelson*

34 YEARS OF MEMORIES

I wish I were a writer! Mary always wanted to sit down with me and write memories ... good and bad. I wish we would have taken the time. I have 34 years of memories. My heart will always be with Mary and Maggie's. I felt blessed to be with Mary when she passed. Peaceful and sad.

A memory I have of working in the kitchen with some really crazy, mischievous people is when one of the prep cooks shared, "How do you tell spaghetti is done? You throw it on the ceiling and if it sticks it's done!" **Right after the cook threw it up on the ceiling, Mary walked in the kitchen to tell me what a good job I did that night.** She stopped right under the spaghetti. I thought I was going to faint, figuring that this was the day I would be fired! As I'm talking to Mary, trying not to look at the ceiling, the spaghetti started to let loose, one noodle at a time, hanging over Mary's head. She said goodnight and turned to walk out the door. The spaghetti held up until just after she left! I recovered and we had a good laugh.

More and more, as I got to know Mary, I know that she would have laughed too.

Another funny memory was my first day bartending. I was so nervous because I was alone at the bar. There was no one to help if I didn't know how to make a drink. I had to wing it. Four people walked in and asked me

Above and at right: Mary Kay DeFoe
Below, right: Mary Kay and Brenda Erickson

if we had good Bloody Marys. I said, "They are the best in town" I loved making them and was so happy when they ordered four. They were masterpieces when I was done. The customers said they were beautiful and the best Bloody Marys they had ever had. I was so excited. They were so good that they ordered four more! I was thrilled and started making them. **That was when I realized that I had forgotten to put vodka in the first ones.** Now, what do I do? The vodka is going to change the taste ... so this time I only put a little vodka in. They said they were wonderful, paid their bill and left a huge tip.

Lutefisk dinners were my favorite night of the year. I didn't have a clue what it was when Debbie Erickson asked me to help her. Little did I know I would be cooking that stinky

fish one night a year for 34 years! The best way to cook it was in the pizza oven on very high heat. We tried deep frying, boiling, broiling, and even making a lutefisk milk shake—Larry's idea to try to make it taste good.

The first taste of lutefisk was good but most couldn't get past a second try. Every time a new employee worked on that night we said it was tradition that they try it and most servings ended up in the garbage. I loved it. Larry and I always shared the first piece. Ed Erickson always watched over us, before and after he passed. We toasted Ed with a shot of akvavit every year.

Mary sure knew how to throw a party. I know she is in charge of entertainment in heaven. We sure are going to miss her.

—Love, Mary Kay DeFoe

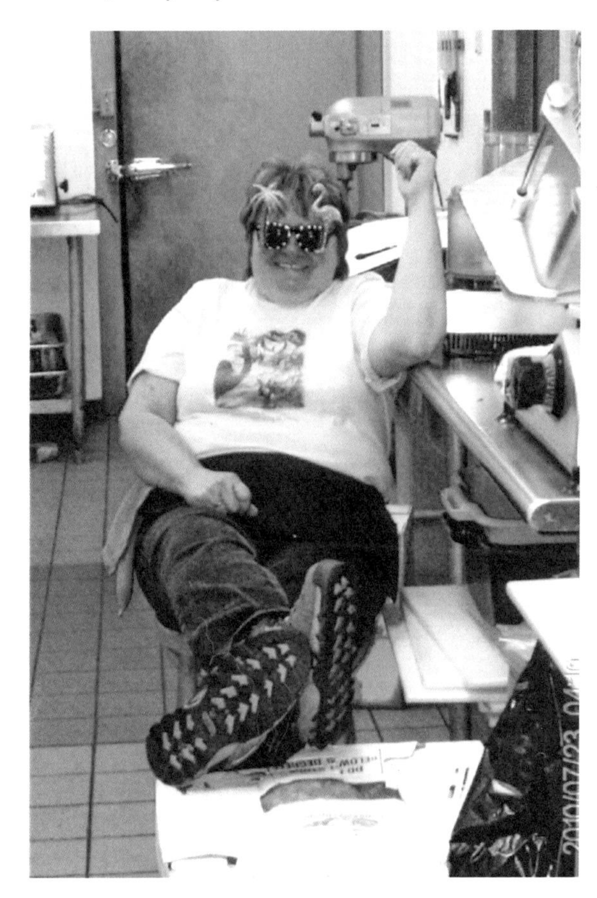

The big bucks!

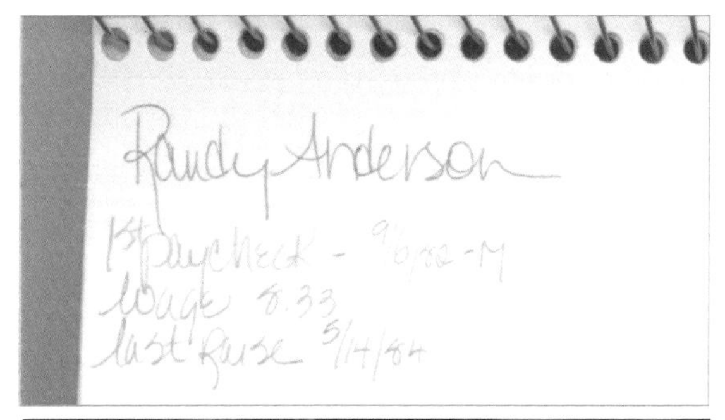

Above: Randy Anderson
At right: Margie Erickson

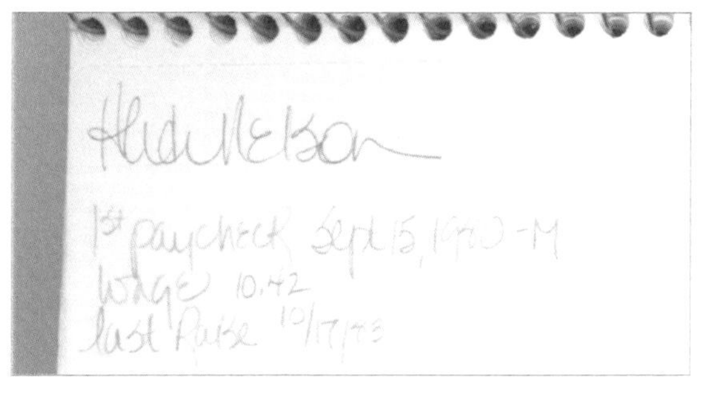

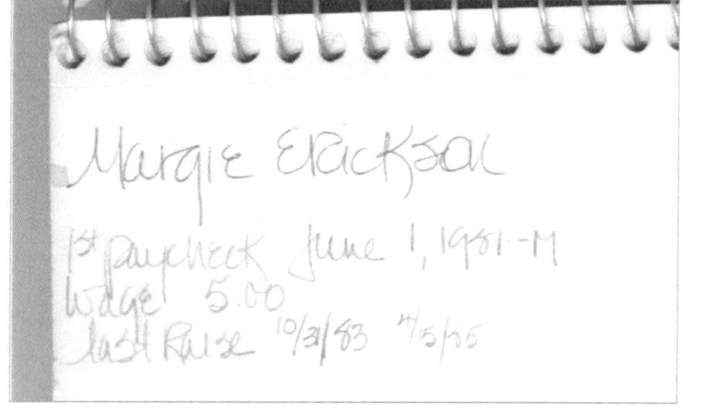

Early days party time

John Hanson "behind the lens"

Early days party time

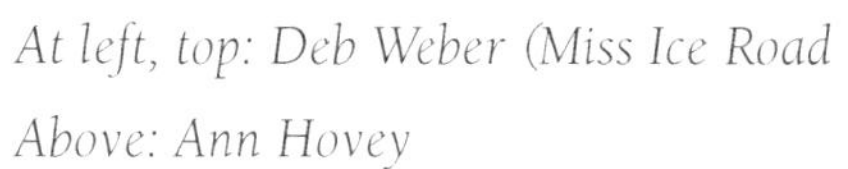

At left, top: Deb Weber (Miss Ice Road

Above: Ann Hovey

Top right: Rick Thompson, unknown

Right:: Keith Oschner

Far right: Chris Meyers

Below right: Janel Ryan (at right) with Julie Zenner

QUARTER-HORSE RACING

I remember eating pizza at Juniors as a child, and participating in "quarter-horse racing" at Maggie's as an adult! Lots of great memories.

—Wendy Frechette Sherburne

Early days party time

Top left: Chris Meyers, Sharon Wszalek, Wayne Barningham. Below left: Janel Ryan.
Above: David Johnson, Ann Hovey, Mary in pink, Diane Brander (hat)
Below: Kim Johnson and Debi Smith's mom, Laura Smith, who worked at the bank
Below right: Bruce Prevost, Jim Hauser, Sharon Wszalek, Keith Eid

Evolving exterior

Below: Todd Burger, Dale Hanson

Janel Ryan: suitable behavior

Having spent a couple summers in Bayfield, I moved to town in August of 1989 with my soon-to-be husband, bought a house, started a B&B, and planned my outdoor wedding in my new yard. Maggie's was deemed the perfect place to have my bachelorette party, so in mid September my girlfriends and I descended on the flamingo palace for dinner and drinks and then more drinks and then "drunk girl dancing" and on into the night. Once recovered, we all laughed at ourselves

Early days in the kitchen

and proclaimed it a night to remember but swore our transgressions to secrecy.

In October I began looking for a job, and was told that Maggie's was looking for a manager and decided to apply. Heidi Nelson approved my application and set up an interview with Mary Rice. I met Mary for the first time at the Knight House and we had a far-ranging chat. Just as I was feeling comfortable with the interview, Mary looked at me and said **"I heard all about your escapades at Maggie's last month and I'm not sure that behavior is suitable for a managerial position."** I sat there unable to speak, wondering exactly what she had heard, and began to stutter a response when Mary burst out laughing and said, "And yet it reminded me of some of my own adventures and I think I will give you the job!" So began a 10-year collaboration with "the Queen" and a wonderful opportunity to become part of this community and to see firsthand all she did for our lovely little town.

Mary never failed to amaze me with her imagination, energy, and ideas, and she pushed me to make Maggie's better every year. She shared her love of food and wine and generously invited me to share some of her adventures in wine country. She was an inspiration to live life fully, to work hard, and to keep pushing the boundaries of what we are capable of. **Thank you Mary, party on!**

My thoughts on the closing of Maggie's ... So many memories come rushing back, so much laughter, so many "hare-brained ideas," so many race weeks complete with quarter-horse racing, additions and remodeling, the fabulous chefs I got to work with, new menus to imagine and refine, and, of course, trying to eat lutefisk once a year. And through it all, Mary cruising through the back door to check in, grab a piece of bacon and head to the "Queen's table". **Perhaps it is fitting that it should end with her.** It will take all of us years to recount the memories. Perhaps when a new owner steps in to begin again they can create their own Bayfield fables. —*Janel Ryan*

Below: Pool table party, 1982. Yes, that's Janel!

Kitchen before 1999 remodel

Top left: Bonita Haskins

Above: Mary Kay Defoe and John Hanson

Below: Larry Soulier

Ethnic dinners

MEXICAN NIGHT AT MAGGIE'S

This Maggie's/Lake Superior tale took place sometime in January of 1982.

I was living on Madeline Island, in what was once a very communal house with an ever-changing roster of residents. The residents on this day consisted of myself, Keith Sowl, and Nick Browne. Nick and Keith were due to leave shortly to pass the rest of the winter in Florida but they were busy trying to scrounge together enough loose change to pay for the gas to get there.

I was the only one gainfully employed at that time. I had a full time, although poorly paid, job at the Madeline Island Yacht Club. Keith was waiting for his unemployment checks to show up and Nick was commercial ice fishing part time with Roy "Cigar" Nelson. Although I didn't pay rent to Keith, who owned the house, I was paying the bills, electric, and LP gas. The house was heated 100% with wood and Keith kept that pretty well supplied. To put it mildly, we were living on a shoestring. Because Nick was fishing with Cigar, our main source of nourishment was fish, fresh from the lake.

Now, I love fresh fish as much as anyone, but when you are eating fish for two meals a day, seven days a week, it gets a little old and the smell of fish oil permeating the kitchen never goes away. It was a cold winter, but as of that week, we hadn't had an ice road, the beer was running out, and the dirty laundry pile was growing larger. I got home from work to find that Keith had made creamed fish on toast for dinner. It probably would have been delicious if we hadn't all eaten fish for the last 35 meals, but I am pretty sure that the dogs, La Mont and Jasmine, ate more of that fish than Nick and I did. Keith, of course, wolfed down his portion.

Word got out the next day, that the ice road was open. Bob Teisberg was our neighbor and had spent many hours with us that winter playing board games and drinking gallon jugs of cheap wine and was apparently with us when the news got out. Keith, Bob, and I decided that we were going to scrape together enough pennies to do some laundry, and buy ourselves a case of the cheapest beer that we could find. Over the ice road we went, in my trusty 1968 Chevy Impala.

We made it to Bayfield without trouble, went to Super Saver to buy our beer and then headed to the laundromat to stuff as many clothes as possible into the washing machines. While we waited for the laundry we decided to head to Maggie's because we had enough money left (or I probably had enough money left) to buy each of us a tap beer.

So there we were, sitting at the bar, nursing our beers, and enjoying a little change of venue and new winter faces.

Keith and Carol Sowl … still on the Island!

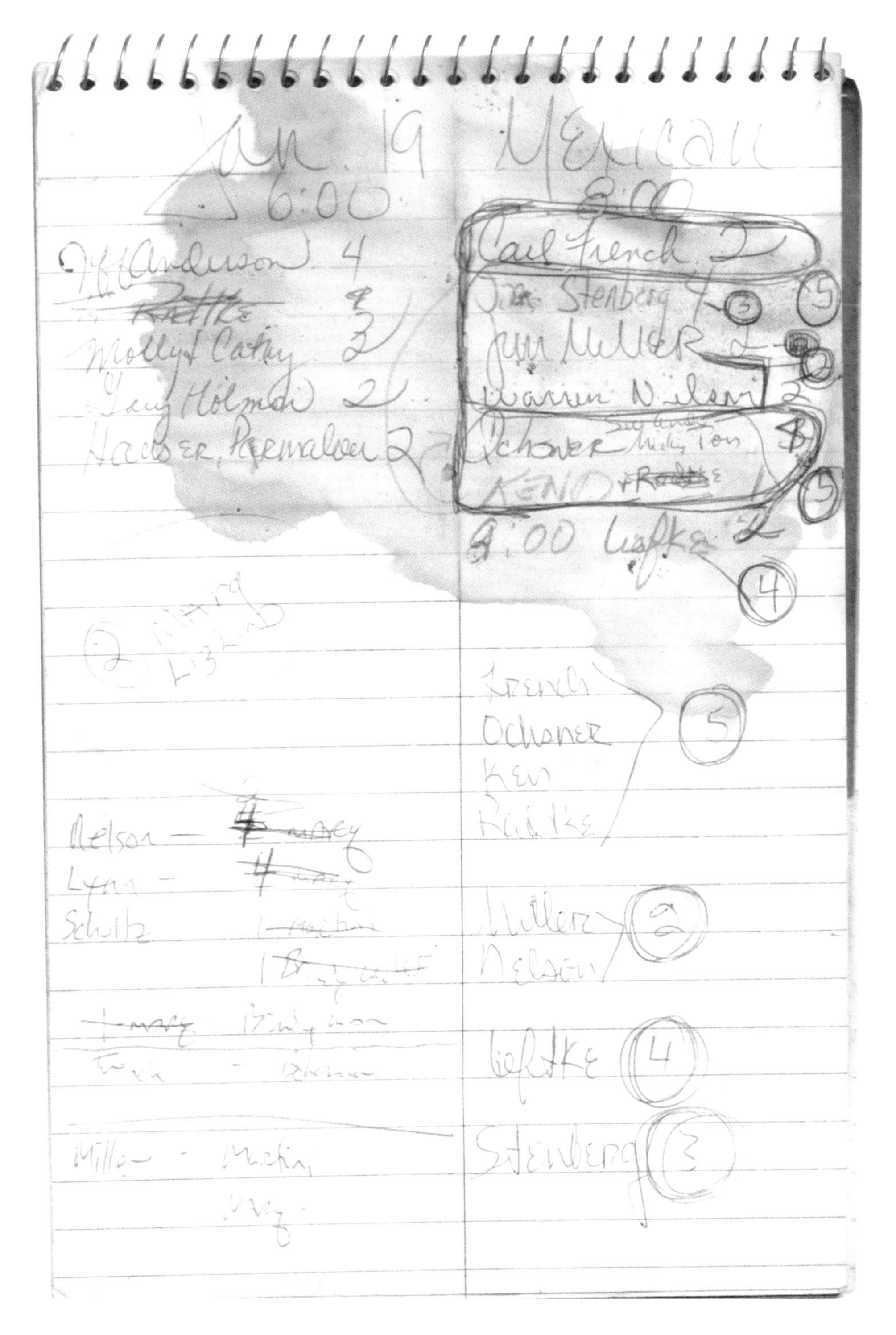

There were some pretty amazing smells coming from the kitchen. Mary came out and greeted us and announced that it was the very first "Mexican Night" at Maggie's. I don't know how badly we were drooling, but am pretty sure that as the plates came out of the kitchen past us on their way to paying customers, there were three sets of eyes that followed each one of those plates to the tables.

Mary finally took pity on us and asked if we would like to order. We mumbled something about being dead broke and **she laughed and told us that she would give us credit until May if we promised that we would pay off our tabs then**. You never saw three servings ordered as quickly and I am pretty sure that those orders also included three margaritas.

We were in culinary heaven as we ate those dinners, so much so that we didn't notice the time and our clothes got locked into the laundromat for the night. As we were finishing up our dinners, Wayne Nelson walked in and told us that **the ice road was candling and it had broken up in a few places.** We thanked our hostess, promised again to pay and hightailed out of there.

The high speed dash across the candling ice, with the Impala's windshield wipers working overtime so that Keith could make his way across the lake, was literally death defying. The engine block of the Impala was caked in ice by the time we got back to the island. **But that was the best Mexican food that I have ever tasted in my life.**

I am happy to say that I paid off my IOU well in advance of the May deadline. I am pretty sure that sometime in May I ended up paying off Keith's as well. Not sure if Teisberg ever paid his off! Thank you, Mary!

—Happily submitted by Carol Sowl

P.S. from Heidi Nelson: "Great story and those first dinners were $5! Deal of a lifetime."

Ethnic dinners

Greetings from Maggie's—Bayfield's one and only shrine to pink flamingos, food, and fun. Although it's winter and you must "watch out where the Huskies go," **you needn't eat that yellow snow cause we're open daily** from 6 a.m. to 9 p.m. (10 p.m. on weekends) serving great homemade meals. Now suppose you're just a little bit thirsty, well we have that covered from our bar, the only one in the area with an overhead train. We serve great cocktails, imported and domestic beers, California wines and special hot drinks to take the chill off. Count on the bar being open late because we consider missing "Cheers" a sacrilege, even though that means struggling through the 'local snooze.'

In ski season, hand your Mt. Ashwabay lift ticket to one of our fine bartenders and have a drink on us. Every Sunday you can cheer on our ice racing team lead by Jim Defoe and his '75 Caddy.

We are spicing up winter with **Ethnic Dinners on Wednesday nights** at least once a month. Included will be Chinese, Mexican, Northern Italian, Greek, and maybe Indonesian. There's more. Every Tuesday night an All-You-Can-Eat Shrimp Feast and on February 14th our own version of "Cupid's Caper, A Culinary Delight" complete with decorations done in Maggie's fashion.

Cast caution aside, come see us, we're a little looney, but you'll love us and you can take home a t-shirt or sweat shirt to prove it.

—As always, your tacky but never tedious friends at Maggie's!

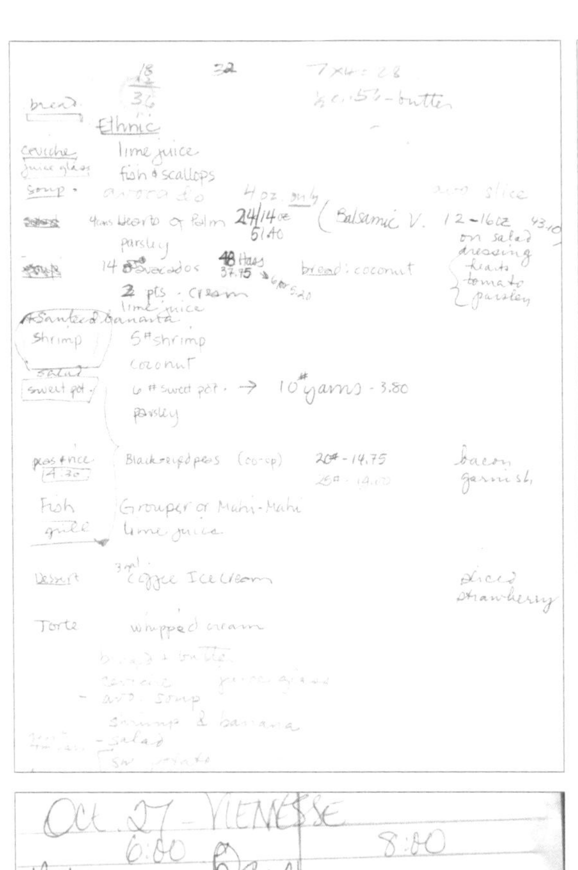

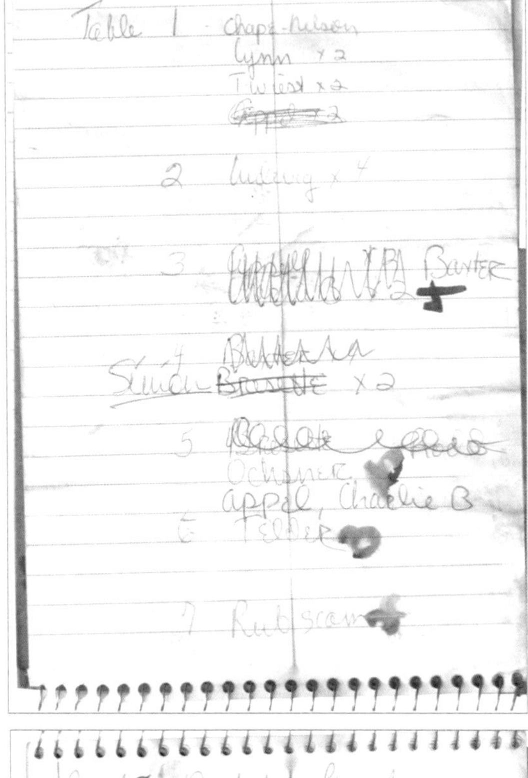

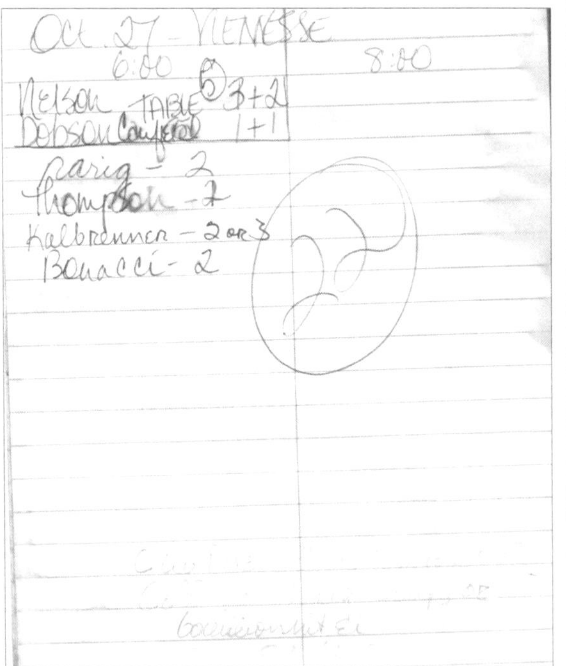

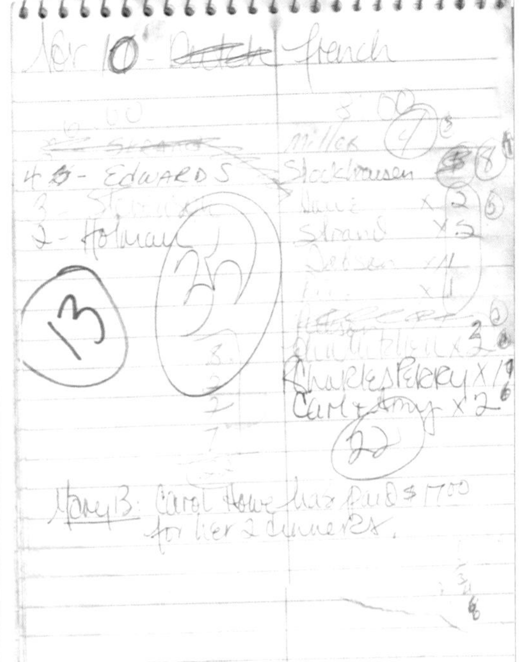

Ethnic dinners

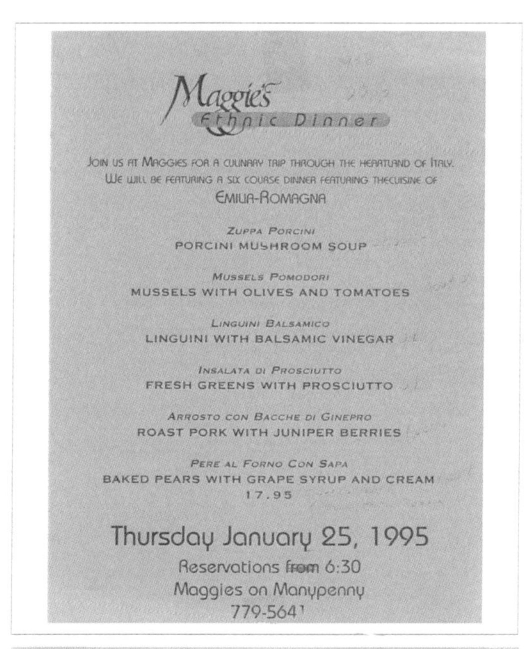

FISH CEVICHE — cozumel, mex.

- chop fish filets or seafood + marinate 2 hrs. in Lime juice
- saute clove of garlic in olive oil - remove garlic, cool oil

mix oil w:
chopped onion
" tomato
" hot pepper
oregano
(ketsup)
s + p.
dash lime juice + water
then add fish.

WALNUT SAUCE
whip cream add:
lemon zest
salt + pepper, men...
coarsely chopped walnuts

S. American
→ Ensalado Olímpica M. 146
Garlic Soup Sopa de Ajó H&S 87
Empanadas - Hot & Spicy p. 210
w/ Pebre Salsa de Cilantro - M. 158
Peruvian Potatos w/ Cheese Sauce H&S 121
✓ Vatapa - H&S 159
✓ Cola de Mono - M.
Vino Caliente
Pear Empanadas Turnovers w/ manjar
✓ manjar

avacados
cilantro
Filo
Dried shrimp

Maggie's Goes South American

Thursday January 23rd ** Two Seatings 6pm & 8:15pm

The Menu ** Argentinian Garlic Soup ** Cauliflower-Avacado Salad from Chile ** Chicken Pasteries from Equador
Brazilian Fish & Seafood Jumble with Peruvian Style Potatoes ** Pear Turnovers with "Cola de Mono" Tail of the Monkey from Bolivia
Reservations ** 779-5641 ** $13.95

Dine on the Orient Express
at Maggie's
February 4, 1993

Schweeberger (2) @ 6:00. 779-3348

Begin your culinary adventure in
Paris, France
and eat your way through
Zurich, Switzerland
Vienna, Austria
Budapest, Hungary
Sofia, Bulgaria & your final repast
Istanbul, Turkey*

22 people
9 at 6
13 at 8:15

2 Departures 6pm & 8:15pm
$14.95 Boarding Passes call 779-5641

*One lucky passenger will receive free boarding for the next Ethnic Dinner March 4

257 Manypenny Bayfield, Wisconsin 54814-0457

Caribbean Night
at
Maggie's

Thursday
March 21st
Two Seatings
6pm & 8:15pm

The Menu
Ceviche
Hearts of Palm Salad
Curried Avocado Soup
Coconut Shrimp
Fresh Fish Caribe'
Jamaica Cafe' & Almond Torte

Plus Rum Bobos at Carnival prices

13.95

Reservations 779-5641

Ethnic dinners

United Nations Nite

Maggie's

The Menu

Black Bean Ful - Middle East

Warm Lamb & Walnut Salad - Australia

Spicy Peanut Chicken Soup - Indonesia

Calamari Frito - Italy

Carne Asada with New Mexico Chili Bread & Creamy Rice - Mexico

Pecan Praline Cheesecake - USA

$13.95 Reservations 779-5641

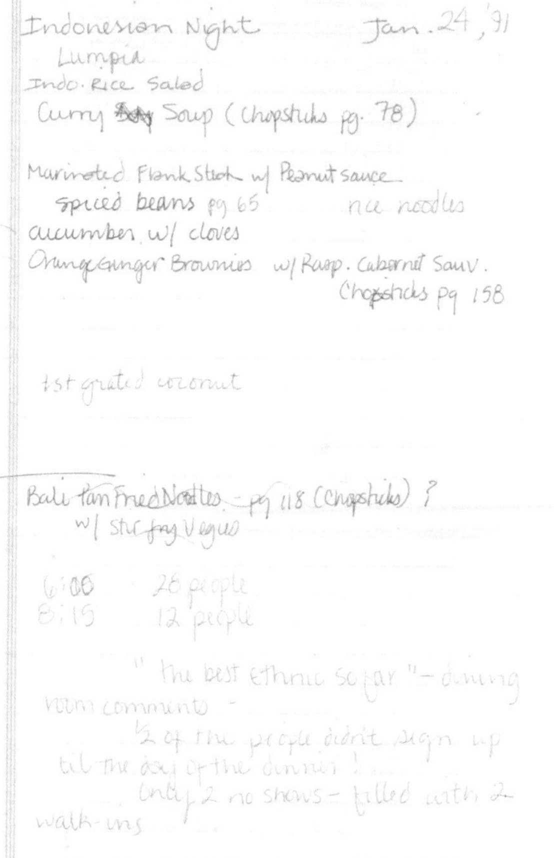

Indonesian Night Jan. 24, '91

Lumpia

Indo. Rice Salad

Curry Soup (Chopsticks pg. 78)

Marinated Flank Steak w/ Peanut sauce

spiced beans pg 65 rice noodles

cucumber w/ cloves

Orange Ginger Brownies w/ Rasp. Cabernet Sauv.

Chopsticks pg 158

1st grated coconut

Bali Pan Fried Noodles - pg 118 (Chopsticks)?

w/ stir fry Veggies

6:00 28 people

8:15 12 people

"the best ethnic so far" - dining room comments -

½ of the people didn't sign up til the day of the dinner!

Only 2 no shows - filled with 2 walk-ins

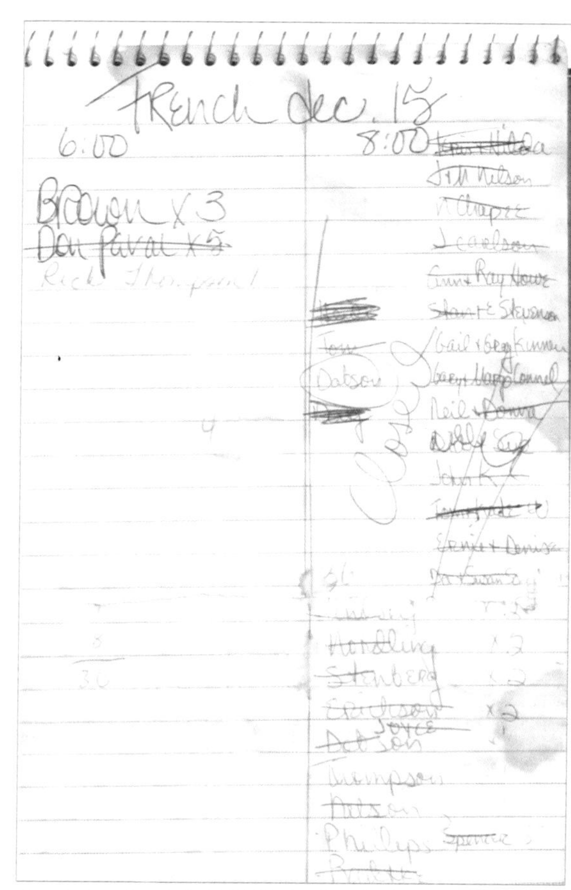

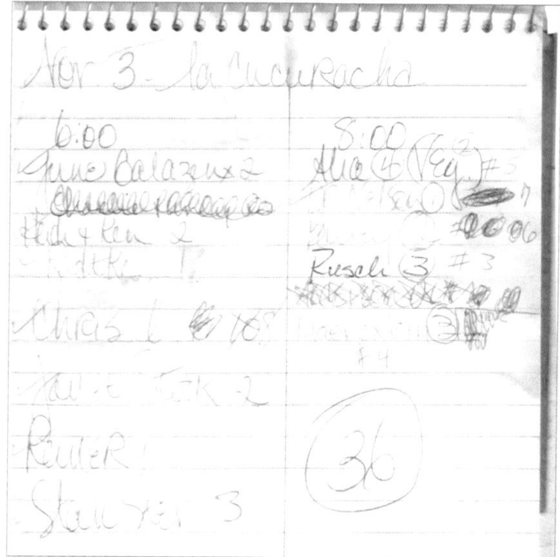

Too much fun!

Hayley Webster, Shannon Anderson, Molly Rice

THE BEST JOB

I started working at Maggie's as a waitress/bartender in 1988. My brother Tim was the night bartender and my co-workers on the floor were Diane and Nancy Erickson. LuLu worked during the day. Mary Kay and Lois worked at night. Lois and I loved playing tunes and sharing our music. Larry and Bonita were the head cooks and Janel Ryan was our manager. Larry served up a lot of "Native American Burgers" with some special sauce. Bonita claimed, each and every morning, that she could never read my chicken scratch. And I can't forget about Bob the Baker who would make special pies just for my shift!

I worked there each summer for about seven years and paid for all my college tuition with that job. We only had nine tables (and the secret appetizer window) and we never had time to rest the whole eight-hour shift! We were lucky to get a bathroom break! The best part of the night was counting tips, telling stories about customers, and **sharing a beer before heading over to Morty's or out on a sailboat for a moonlight sail.**

It was the best job and I still dream of it and wish for those days again. I am so grateful for my opportunities at Maggie's!

—*Patsy Olson Zemke*

APPLE FEST PARADE TAILGATING

We always gathered at the intersection on top of the hill near the church parking lot where Maggie's float was staged. Karlyn Holman and The Apple Core crew were next to us with plenty of drink and snacks to share. Excitement was in the air after a long summer of working hard catering to tourists wound down. A bonus was that it was Sunday and Mary always closed Maggie's that day.

For several years Phil Sunde (Tiny) and I were in charge of hooking up Maggie's multi-colored beaded, bathtub car/float and hauling it to the starting line. We felt pressure to make sure we were in the right spot, lined up correctly, and knew the timing of when to "go." We had a ladder for Mary so she could climb into the bathtub and it was my task to help her negotiate the tricky steps.

This is where the funny part happens that I will never forget. It was not long after Mary had been recovering from knee surgery and we were all concerned if she should attempt to do this. But you know her! "Let's do it," she said. Picture me leading her up the ladder, step one, two, three … Okay, we got this.

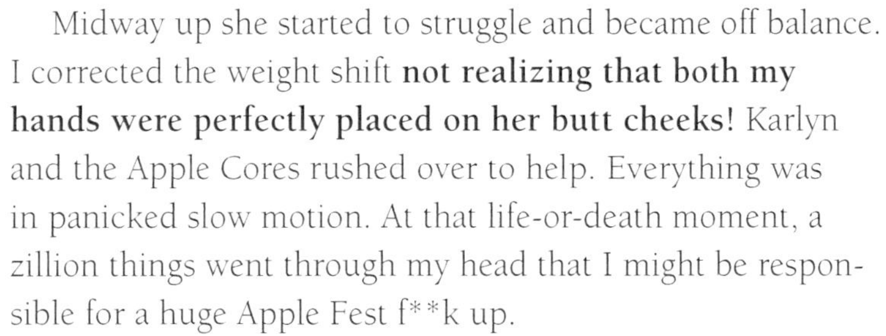

Midway up she started to struggle and became off balance. I corrected the weight shift **not realizing that both my hands were perfectly placed on her butt cheeks!** Karlyn and the Apple Cores rushed over to help. Everything was in panicked slow motion. At that life-or-death moment, a zillion things went through my head that I might be responsible for a huge Apple Fest f**k up.

Mary said "**Push my butt like you mean it Nick**, I'm getting in that tub !" With those words she gave me the strength and I finished the task; mission accomplished.

Later, Mary looked me in the eye and we shared a very special wordless moment realizing how embarrassing that must have looked but we didn't care because we knew we had each other's back. —*Nick Lunde*

20 — THE DAILY PRESS — Ashland, WI — Monday, October 4, 2004

Up North Images

TRAVELING WITH STYLE — A traffic head-turner, this whimsical conveyance was the preferred method of travel for Bayfield free spirit Mary Rice who along with her pet pooch Max, got an opportunity to greet the Applefest parade crowd from the vantage of her car-topping bathtub.

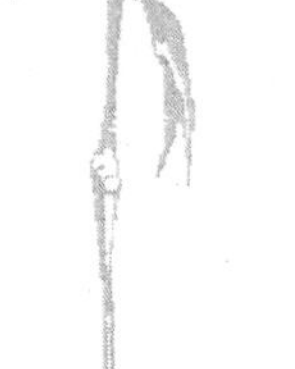

apple fest breakfast

apple pancakes-three cakes topped with glazed apple slices, sausage or bacon----4.50
fisherman's special-two eggs, sausage or bacon, american fries, toast and jelly----4.50
logger's special-three buckwheat pancakes, two eggs, sausage or bacon---------4.00

#1------one egg, toast and jelly-----1.55
#2----- two eggs, toast and jelly-----2.15
#3------one egg, sausage or bacon, toast and jelly-----3.00
#4----- two eggs, sausage or bacon, toast and jelly-----3.60
#5----- homemade apple muffin-----1.00

bayfield apple cider-----.75 and 1.00
coffee-----.75
decafe-----.75
tea-----.60
cocoa-----.60
milk-----.65 and 1.15
juices-----1.25 and 1.95

buy an apple fest raffle ticket
and leave bayfield with an extra five grand

no substitutions
no separate checks please

Back row, l-r: Leslie Falconer, Andrea Falconer, Essie Marzolf, Jan Esposito, Deb Weber, unknown, Karlyn Holman. Front row, l-r: : Marcie Gephardt, Terri Wagner

STARTERS

ONION RINGS 9.00
crispy panko crusted onions,
Maggie's dipping sauces

ELLSWORTH CHEESE CURDS 9.75
crispy fried white cheddar curds,
roasted garlic aioli

POTATO SKINS 8.50 **HALF ORDER** 5.00
bacon, cheddar jack, green onions, sour cream

TOTCHOS 11.00
crispy seasoned tator tots, chorizo sausage, jalapeño
cheese sauce, lettuce, tomatoes, black olives,
green onions

FLAMINGO TENDERS 9.25
deep fried chicken breast strips in hot cayenne pepper
sauce, side of blue cheese dressing

BLACK BEANS AND RICE 7.00
cheddar jack, green onions, pico de gallo, sour cream

SOUPS

Please check our dining room chalkboards for the daily offerings in either a cup or a bowl.

SOUP OF THE DAY 3.25 **Cup** 4.75 **Bowl**

MAGGIE'S CHILI 3.50 **Cup** 5.00 **Bowl**

SALADS

choice of Maggie's blue cheese, ranch, italian, 1000 island, raspberry-balsamic dressing or vinegar and oil.

MIXED BABY GREENS 6.50
organic baby greens, onions, carrots,
tomatoes and cucumbers

MAGGIE'S APPLE ORCHARD SALAD 12.00
baby greens, onions, toasted almonds,
fresh Bayfield apples with house made
poppy seed dressing

SOUTHWESTERN CAESAR SALAD 9.75
romaine lettuce, spicy chipotle-lime dressing,
parmesan, crispy tortilla strips
with grilled chicken 12.25

BLACK 'N BLUE CHICKEN SALAD 12.75
cajun seasoned char-grilled chicken breast on organic
baby greens, tomatoes, cucumbers, red onions,
bacon and blue cheese dressing

On Tap

PREMIUM ON DRAUGHT
12 oz - 5.00 Pint - 6.00 Pitcher - 16.00

Bayfield Apfelhaus Cidery
Blueberry Hard Cider

Central Waters *Octoberfest*

Earth Rider *Caribou Lake*

Milwaukee *Outboard*

Sierra Nevada *Hazy IPA*

CHAR-GRILLED BURGERS

Maggie's uses USDA Choice 7 oz. burger patties served on a brioche bun. All burgers include potato chips and a pickle.

substitute - home-cut fries 2.50
substitute - sweet potato fries 3.50
substitute - onion rings 4.50

add - California style - lettuce, tomato, onion 1.50
add - gluten-free bun 1.25
add additional side - Maggie's dipping sauces .50 each
creamy tarragon or secret sauce

ALL-AMERICAN BURGER 10.00
Apple smoked bacon and aged cheddar

BAYFIELD BURGER 11.00
Grilled burger topped with apple chutney
and cheddar cheese

BLACK'N BLUE BURGER 9.00
cajun seasoned burger with blue cheese
and Maggie's secret dipping sauce

Burgers cooked rare, medium rare or pink in the middle may be undercooked and are served only upon request.

NOT BURGERS

CHICKEN FAJITA 13.00
garlic-lime marinated chicken breast, grilled onions
and peppers, tortillas, black beans and rice, lettuce,
cheddar jack, black olives, pico de gallo, sour cream

CHIPOTLE BLACK BEAN VEGGIE BURGER 10.50
lettuce, tomato, onion, roasted garlic aioli,
chips and a pickle

NIGHT TIME ENTREES

night time entrees are available after 4:30 p.m. and include an organic baby greens salad, choice of dressing, bread included by request.

WARM SICILIAN PASTA 13.00 with **CHICKEN** 16.50
fettuccine tossed with olive oil, sautéed garlic,
tomatoes, Kalamata olives, feta and basil

PORK LOIN 19.00
roasted pork loin, apple chutney, stuffing,
roasted potatoes

PIZZAS

THE LATE NIGHT SPECIAL 9" 11.00 12" 15.00
pesto, chicken, tomato, parmesan, feta

THE NAPA VALLEY 9" 11.50 12" 15.50
olive oil, chicken, brie, caramelized onions,
roasted red peppers, parmesan

MAGGIE'S HOUSE 9" 12.00 12" 16.00
pizza sauce, green olives, green peppers,
onions, tomatoes, pepperoni, italian
sausage, mozzarella

DESSERTS

CARAMEL APPLE CHEESECAKE 6.50
CARAMEL APPLE SUNDAE 6.00
APPLE CRISP 6.00
APPLE CAKE 6.50
APPLE PIE 6.50
LAVA CAKE 7.00
BROWNIE 5.50

Maggie's WELCOMES YOU TO THE 58th
ANNUAL APPLE FESTIVAL
257 Manypenny Avenue
Bayfield, WI. 54814
715-779-5641
maggies-bayfield.com

The people make it happen

SPONGE BOB AS GUEST CONDUCTOR

I was Maggie's bartender occasionally and also night cleaner. On slow days behind the bar, my eyes wandered over all the cool stuff on the walls: paintings, photos, and knickknacks. The model train above my head fascinated me most. Hmmm …

A day or so later, I was on night cleaner shift which was usually from about midnight to 4:00 a.m. I had the whole place to myself, jamming to tunes as I swept and mopped. Again the train caught my eye and a plan formulated. There were plenty of flamingos everywhere but I need to add a "touch of Nick." It would be somewhat discreet, or so I thought. I had a Sponge Bob figurine that fit perfectly in the caboose of the train and I propped him in there as my own private joke, not telling anyone.

Unbelieveably, it wasn't noticed for a couple weeks until one day as I was bartending, a cute little girl asked me to turn on the Sponge Bob Train. I did so and she was delighted, cheering "Sponge Bob Sponge Bob!" Mary happened to be eating there at the time and she noticed how excited the girl was about the train. I remember Mary walking over to their table and saying "Sponge Bob?" The wide-eyed girl pointed at the train. Mary followed her gaze to the train, and at the same time, me behind the bar wondering if I had broken the "flamingo décor" rules. Mary let out a boisterous "All right!"

From thinking I was in trouble one second, (in my head of course), to being praised by Mary the next made me melt with pride. She loved it!

—Nick Lunde

Jan26 - Feb 2

	Bar		Kitchen	
26	Heidi Sharon	Cindy	Karen	Henry
27	Heidi	Cindy	Karen	Sharon
28	Heidi	Kevin	Karen	Sharon
29	Cindy	Scotty	Karen	Henry
30	Heidi	Tim	Cindy	Sharon
31	Cindy	Bill	Sharon	Karen
1st 32	Heidi	Kevin	Mary	Henry

HOMEMADE APPLE PIES

While Wild Rice was being built, I worked at Maggie's as bartender, bringing some of my loyal Morty's Pub customers with me. One in particular was Diane Weber, a second mom to me. On slow afternoons at Morty's, Diane would come in specifically because she knew I was bartending. We had a shared passion for watching cooking shows, sharing recipes, great chefs—Julia Child, Anthony Bourdain—usually just the two of us on a lazy afternoon enjoying a shared passion.

Morty's closed for a bit and I went to Maggie's. Diane and I had just started to get to know each other so it was a bit of a shock to our routine. I invited her to visit me although it would be different with no TV, pool table, or jukebox, but she said she loved the food and would definitely stop by. And she did, several times. We were back to normal, in a different way.

On one particularly busy early evening at Maggie's, when customers were overflowing the deck and lined up outside the door, Diane walked in with a box in her arms. She wriggled through the crowd and miraculously found a seat at the bar. Through the chaos of tourists, my bartender eyes noticed my sweet Diane and I dropped what I was doing to greet her.

She quickly ordered a drink, understanding that I was "in the weeds," and sat back to enjoy the show of tourist restaurant madness. She conversed with people siting next to her and after finding out she was a local they asked the usual questions. Gracefully, Diane shared her knowledge but I saw that she was really missing talking to me!

Nick Lunde

That's when she picked up the box she had sitting on the floor and put it on the bar, calling me over. "Nick," she said. "These are the honey crisp apple pies I promised you and Phil." She winked sweetly at me and was out the door.

Immediately tourists at the bar were asking about the box of homemade apple pies that had just landed in front of them. A hilarious bidding war began! I ended the auction for Diane's made-with-love apple pies by saying, "These apple pies are not for sale!" and the next day I scarfed down a whole pie.

—*Nick Lunde*

CUSTOMERS ... GOTTA LOVE 'EM!

Senator Russ Feingold came in one afternoon and started moving tables around to seat his large group. Not knowing who he was, I stopped him and told him that he had to wait out on the patio just like everyone else!

Patty Olson Zemke

Roger Bristol, who regularly came in for lunch, usually a bowl of soup, would leave a nickel for a tip. At the end of the summer I would get a $5 bill.

When I worked there, Maggie's was famous for our fresh margaritas and Bloody Marys because we did not use a mix. We also had a *huge* beer list and spectacular wine list that brought the meals to another level.

While bartending, a regular customer "all the way from Thunder Bay" used to watch me. One night he proclaimed that he wished he was my dog, "so I could lick all that spilled alcohol off of you."

—*Patty Olson Zemke*

MYSTERY TOURS

Magical mystery tours were another one of Mary's crazy adventures with all the staff. A bus would pick us up at Maggie's parking lot. The only thing she would tell us is how to dress and how long we would be gone. Every tour was different but full of crazy fun! Lots of alcohol was involved and great food!

—*Mary Kay Defoe*

FABULOUS FOR KIDS!

The best thing about Maggie's for us was a great place to take kids. The flamingos everywhere, the booths, the staff, the train, and of course the amazing hot chocolate in the best mugs on the planet. It was fabulous for kids!

—*Liz Woodworth*

The people make it happen

WORK FELT LIKE COMING HOME

I didn't start my journey as a Maggie's employee in the traditional sense of seeking a job but I'm so glad I had the opportunity to work for such an iconic Bayfield eatery. I truly enjoyed being part of the flamingo family! My daughter had worked at Maggie's for several seasons and in the summer of 2017 she had the chance to travel to Australia. Many of you know that in a touristy town it's often tough to find people to cover shifts mid-season. We had worked very hard for the "Jossie to Aussie" campaign so I came in to the pretty pink restaurant on the corner of 3rd and Manypenny to assist in covering shifts while Joslyn was away. Little did I know how my life would change and that I'd love so much about Maggie's.

It was such a pleasure to "work" for a company that really knew how to treat their employees. Work never felt like work. Work felt more like coming home to visit with your favorite friends and family—just sometimes that included 500 or so guests too! I will forever be indebted to Maggie's. Not only was this the best place to eat in town, with the best customer service providers, **it was where my daughter learned how to use a washing machine!** Thank you Mary and a thousand thank yous to the visitors and most excellent co-workers I've ever had.

—*Crystal Newago*

BLESSING FOR A SMALL TOWN

I started washing dishes at Maggie's in 1980 or 81; not sure. **My first night was an ethnic dinner night.** I do not recall the theme. **I do know that I washed every dish by hand!** There was no commercial machine; I did it all in the sink. I was grateful that the restaurant was quite small! Mary herself was cooking along with Jack Gunderson. I really enjoyed getting to know them both. I did a few of the ethnic nights and bussed on busy weekends. Eventually this became a summer job. I was a high school-aged young man and enjoyed working with people older than myself who were supportive and helped me with work ethics and how working together makes the entire operation run smoother. Some cooks I worked with were Cindy Kovachevich, Sharon Wszalek, and Randy Anderson. Randy and I became dedicated listeners to Milwaukee Brewers games on the little transistor radio in the kitchen. My brother Tim bartended there forever. I would have my hands in the sink diligently washing dishes when he would yell my name. I would look up to see a glass flying in my direction from down the hall. With soapy hands I would catch it and put it in line to be washed and he would have a big smile.

I really enjoyed working there. Not many high school kids can have a dishwashing job where they hang out with **"adults" (I use that term loosely).** My friends were jealous that I wanted to go to work every night.

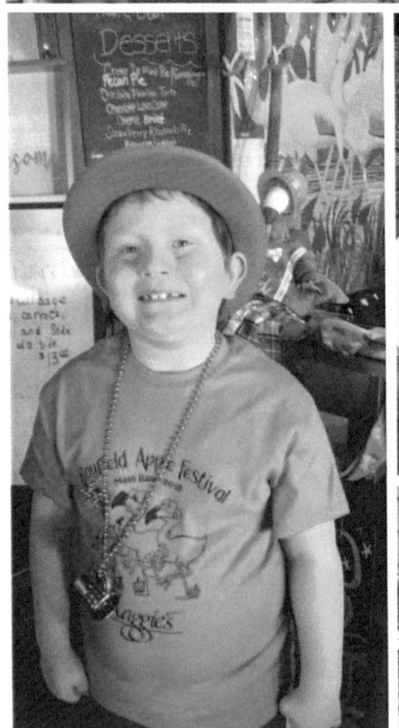

Myles Newago-Howe, Crystal's son

I remember that Sharon Wszalek waited tables and I think that Deb Bresette and Mary Bresette were also waitresses. I think fondly of all the people I worked with.

Once Cindy Kovachevich was using a fancy new kitchen tool—a Cuisinart—to chop cabbage. When it was full, neither she, or I, or Tim, or anybody in the restaurant could get the lid off so we put it in the fridge and tried again the next day. The lid stayed stuck. We called the company and **when they did not help, we sent it (full of three-day-old cabbage) to them. I can only imagine the smell when it arrived.**

As a high school-aged male, I ate constantly. I would make myself a massive pizza and eat it all. The business was small enough that everyone could eat one meal at work and I certainly ate my share.

I need to mention Heidi Nelson, what a shining star in the operation! She was always so positive. It's difficult to really express what her energy added to the place. **Honestly, everybody was positive and wanted the best for customers and each other.**

Of course there was plenty of late night pool table dancing, etc. I am sure you have more colorful stories than what I have provided but perhaps mine helps fill in some of the blanks. I stopped working there in 1982 and, of course, I was a patron of Maggie's for many more years. Mary was so generous to the community–constantly loaning "the burban" (brown Chevrolet Suburban) to anybody who needed it. My parents and their friends drove it to Sun Valley, Idaho for skiing and stayed in her condo there—all for free. What a blessing for a small town.

—Doug Olson

I MET MY HUSBAND AT THE BAR

I started work at Maggie's in 1981-ish when I was 16. I was a dishwasher and prep cook/pizza maker. I worked with Debbie, Sharon, Cathy, Tim, Irene, Cindy, and Heidi; probably more I can't remember. Cindy was a knife thrower. I learned to duck pretty fast. And, I learned that "fuck" was a word used preceding most people's names!

I finally graduated to waitress when I was 18. I think we only had five or six tables but I have never walked so much, and this was before Fitbits! We had so many people standing in line during the movie production (In 1990s a travel video crew filmed a show for broadcast in the U.K.), sailing regattas, and on rainy days. I attended college at UW Lacrosse, then came back and worked summers. I met my now husband at the bar. Robert Goodlet "Bobby" danced and stripped on the pool table for me when I dared him. We started dating because of Maggie's. He visited me at college and proposed. Six months later we were married outside in the Bayfield park.

—Gretchen (Morgan) and Bobby Goodlet

The people make it happen

Ice races. Kenny Dobson in car, Kevin Caufield, Mary in the lounge chair

STORIES FROM A POTTER

I lived in Bayfield from 1979 to 1981 and met Mary in 1980 at a party at the Knight House where she had moved with her two daughters. Mary became a really good friend and we would hang out on different occasions.

One summer afternoon in 1980 when we were driving around in my pickup, she informed me that she had bought Juniors Bar. I said, "Wow, congratulations" and she told me that I was to be a bartender. I protested that I did not know how to bartend and she informed me that it didn't matter! She repeated her "command" and again I told her that I didn't want to be a bartender to which she responded that I was going to be! Long story short: I became a bartender at the yellow Formica bar when she opened Maggie's, pale in comparison to what it became.

In the summer we often closed Maggie's and drove to Little Sand Bay where Mary's boat waited to take us to Sand Island and continue our party. Everyone spent the night.

Another custom that began in that first year was Ethnic Monday Night. Each Monday the cook created dishes from a different part of the world. (On some Mondays it did not go over very well.) The Blue Moon Ball also began at Maggie's. We all dressed in tuxes and formal gowns. When Mary opened the Clubhouse on Madeline Island—a more upscale restaurant—she brought her whole staff to the Twin Cities to show them what good service was. Everyone was put up at the St. Paul Hotel and went to five, high-end restaurants. I was lucky to be on that excursion even though I was not going to be working at Maggie's. In 1981, Mary wanted to open an artist guild. Lisa Spencer and I pulled together a group of artists and opened the Bayfield Artists Guild. Mary was a huge supporter of the arts. Bayfield is what it is now because of her. She helped many artists get a start. She was a great patron and supported my effort to becoming a full time potter. **Thanks, Mary**.

—*Kevin Caufield*

We drank, laughed, and played pool late into the night of my sister's wedding ... she let me win because I was a poor college student.

—*Peter Walters*

JUST LIKE CHEERS

So many memories, where to start? In the "good old days" we packed the diners in for burgers and burger wannabes. The wait staff made the burger patties—every day! They were based on a country theme: Germany, France, Denmark, and more. Each came with a different type of deep-fried potato side. Homemade pies by Uni were fresh daily: huge pieces with tons of ice cream.

Maggie's was like Cheers; you never went in there and didn't know someone! We loved to go for birthdays, order a dessert with a candle and get the place singing Happy Birthday. (Certain people being celebrated were less enthusiastic than the singers.)

Chalkboards typically used for desserts, specials, and soup were great for lively, late-night Pictionary. Perhaps a sampling of refreshments involved, but most of the time we left before it got light out in the morning.

Race week brought crazy antics such as barstool races: pushing barstools across the floor with someone sitting on one made for a vibrating sensation not soon forgotten! Quarter horse races: **place a quarter in your butt crack, hold it in place, race to a cup of beer, drop it in the cup, drink the beer and hold the quarter in your teeth to be the winner!** If that wasn't exciting enough, trading pants and skirts between the sexes just to even things up was a tradition. So many more; probably can't share with polite company. —*Michelle Shrider*

SUMMER ROUTINE: TUESDAY NIGHT TAKE OUT FROM MAGGIE'S

A good routine strenghtens and renews a person. Maggie's is that. Every Tuesday evening my husband, Jim, returns to Bayfield having spent five days on Raspberry Island as the Lighthouse Keeper. The Apostle Island Express docks and there he is, all smiles, Ranger Jim, home from the sea.

Grabbing his gear, we head home to our Manypenny House, formerly Mary's offices for Flamingos Up North. Thrilled to catch up as there is no cell service on Raspberry, we jabber away.

Phoning Maggie's, we place our orders: Grilled Whitefish Sandwich for Jim. Black and Blue Chicken for Jessica with double blue cheese. Most Tuesdays, Maggie's recognizes Jim's voice with a "Hey, Jim, the usual?" which tickles us to no end.

Cocktails on the deck while we wait. We avoid the long lines and eat al fresco on our beautiful porch overlooking Maggie's, the lumber yard, the harbor and Madeline Island; enjoying another gorgeous evening.

Watching the lines of tourists at Maggie's' growing longer and longer, we chuckle, knowing our delicious meal is cooking. The aromas waft up to the deck.

Finally it's time for Jim to "roll down the hill" to Maggie's. Oh golly, what hard work. Nancy or Mary Kay hail Ranger Jim to the bar where our order awaits. Jim touches the

old paycheck window as he pays. From our kitchen, Grandma Cadotte used to watch the lumbermen pick up their paychecks at that small window which was on the exterior of what is now Maggie's.

Tourist heads turn! "Who is that?" they cry. **He who gets to go to the head of the line** and carries his food out through the mob?

Enviously, the outside line watches him quick step up the hill with the crisp white paper bags. He winds through our wild pink rose bushes from our friend Mary, given to

Top: Jim Stowell, aka "Ranger Jim" with John Hanson
Above: Jessica Zuehlke

us on Sand Island. Up the back walk I see the top of his cap climbing the brownstone steps carved by our good buddy Roger Bristol, also a previous owner of this house.

We unpack Tiny's (Phil Sunde) delicious cooking. Our delicious "Every Tuesday Night Summer Routine Take-Out From Maggie's" is a celebration of which we never tire. It unites us as a couple, but more than that, it unites us with the history of this home, this area, and these friends and food we love so deeply.

The best routine for 16 years. Thank you, Mary and Maggie's!

—Jessica Zuehlke

The people make it happen

LUTEFISK AT MAGGIE'S

My first visit to what became Maggie's was when I was taken to the bar—then Juniors Bar owned by Junior Yeska—for a beer by my father-in-law in what had to have been 1960 or 1961. In that time it had not yet been enlarged to its present size, a remodeling project, I believe, taken on by Todd Bonney. Junior Yeska (I believe he lived upstairs) was tending bar.

Howard and Marlene Paap

Benny Montreal was the night watchman at the Allwood Plywood Plant in Bayfield when I worked there in the summer of 1961. He would "swamp-out" Juniors Bar on Sunday mornings. He entered by the rear/side door to clean before it opened for the new week's crowd.

The last Maggie's lutefisk dinner I was part of was in 2019 when my wife and I invited a Red Cliff cousin, Debra Newago, and her friend Penny to join us. This was the first time either of these ladies had ever been in the place.

I learned to enjoy lutefisk at Maggie's. I had eaten it once before, at a Lutheran church basement but like many others turned my nose up at it until nearly 50 years later.

Jimmy and Len Erickson told me of how the tradition began. The Erickson family, in the late 1800s had dried planks of codfish shipped to Bayfield where Jimmy's grandfather soaked them in water to renew them and his wife Christine prepared the dinner. This was for, as Jimmy put it, "The Norwegian fishermen who were alone and had nowhere to go for a holiday dinner came to the Erickson house."

Thanks to Maggie's I now actually enjoy eating a slab or two of lutefisk.

—*Howard Paap*

Editor's note: Thankfully, Mary and Ed Erickson kept the tradition alive: a free holiday lutefisk dinner and wonderful community get-together. They switched paying for it from year to year and Mary took that over when Ed passed on.

At left: Jimmy Erickson with a lutefisk dinner

"O LUTEFISK"

Lutefisk... O Lutefisk... how fragrant your aroma
O Lutefisk... O Lutefisk... You put me, in a coma
You smell so strong... You look like glue
You taste yust like an overshoe
Put Lutefisk ... come Saturday
I tink I'll eat you anyway.

Lutefisk ... O Lutefisk ... I put you by the doorway
I vanted you to ripen up ... yust like dey do in Norway
A dog came by and sprinkled you ... I hit him vit an army shoe
O Lutefisk ... now I suppose
I'll eat you as I hold my nose.

Lutefisk ... O Lutefisk ... how well I do remember
On Christmas Eve how we'd receive ... our big treat of December
It vasn't turkey or fried ham ... it vasn't even pickled spam
My mudder knew dere vas no risk ...
In serving buttered lutefisk.

Lutefisk ... O Lutefisk ... now everyone discovers
Dat Lutefisk and lefse makes-Norweigians better lovers
Now all da vorld can have a ball ... you're better dan dat Yeritol
O Lutefisk ... vit brennevin
You make me feel like Errol Flynn.

Lutefisk ... O lutefisk ... You have a special flavor
Lutefisk ... O lutefisk ... All good Norwegians savor.
That slimy slab we know so well ... Identified by ghastky smell
Lutefisk ... O lutefisk ... Our loyalty won't waver.

Ed's annual lutefisk dinner

At right: 2002 lutefisk menu (kitchen) notes

Below: Chris Pederson at a lutefisk dinner

Middle bottom: Mary leading the singing of O'Lutefisk; words at upper right. Sung to the tune of "O Christmas Tree."

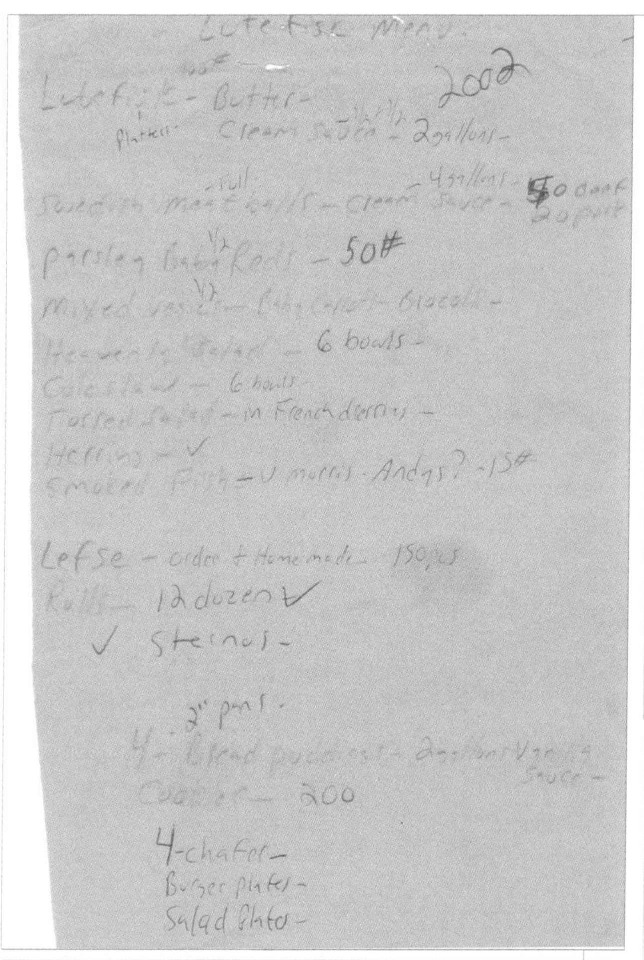

Lutefisk Menu.

2002

Lutefisk – Butter –
Platters Cream Sauce – 2 gallons –

Swedish meatballs – Cream Sauce – 4 gallons – 50
20

Parsley Baby Reds – 50#

Mixed veg – Baby Carrots – Brocolli –

Heavenly Salad – 6 bowls –

Cole slaw – 6 bowls –

Tossed Salad – in French dressing –

Herring – ✓
Smoked Fish – Andys? – 15#

Lefse – order + Homemade – 150 pcs

Rolls – 12 dozen ✓

✓ Sternos –

2" pans –
4 – Bread puddings – 2 gallons Vanilla Sauce –
Cookies – 200

4 – chafer –
Burger plates –
Salad plates –

O' Lutefisk O'Lutefisk

It's the most wonderful
smell of the year!

FOREVER ED'S
LUTEFISK

with all the fixings
and plenty of meatballs!

THURSDAY - DECEMBER 13
Doors open at 5:00 p.m.

Maggie's

O' Lutefisk O'Lutefisk

FOREVER ED'S LUTEFISK

In the spirit of the season
a donation to the
Bayfield Area Food Shelf
would be most appreciated.

257 Manypenny Avenue Bayfield 779-5841

The people make it happen

WOODEN NICKELS!

Mary Rice always looked for occasions to celebrate, and I was fortunate to be included in many of them over the years. I have four wooden nickels that were given out at the 10th Anniversary of Maggie's. What fun!

—Lois Albrecht

WE ASKED LOCALS WHERE TO GO

I first heard of Maggie's in 2003 when I did a Northwoods Bike Tour from Wautoma to Washburn. We stayed in schools or camped in schoolyards and biked to our destination the next day. The final day in Washburn the town sent a shuttle to take us as far as Bayfield and the Big Top. Exploring Bayfield, we asked locals where to go and more than one said "Maggie's" where we were hooked with the fun, meals, and the small size. Waiting outside we met other bikers (pedal bikes) and tourists. The whitefish was a favorite of mine. Nancy was our waitress.

I was so taken that later I brought my wife to Bayfield for a vacation. We stayed a Gruenke's but for sure did a few meals at Maggie's. There

50 WAYS TO USE YOUR T-SHIRT

MAGGIES Lunch 2003

1.) give one to a friend. 2.) use it to wash your car. 3.) wear it as a nightie. 4.) use it to shine your wine glasses. 5.) make a bed for your cat. 6.) use it for a car mat. 7.) shine up your china. 8.) win a wet t-shirt contest. 9.) buy a dozen and sew a quilt. 10.) wear it to maggies and pretend you are an employee. 11.) use it as a fish net. 12.) start a bonfire. 13.) carpet your bathroom. 14.)makes a great fly swatter. 15.) give it to the shirtless guy trying to get into the grocery store. 16.) cut it up to make a rag rug. 17.) sew 100 new dresses for your barbie. 18.) use it as a bib for the slob in your party. 19.) use it to level your table. 20.) makes a great hammock for a baby 21.) use it to stuff your bra. 22.) use it as a bushel basket for your fresh picked bayfield apples. 23.) scalp it on the corner for an extra 5 bucks. 24.) makes a great pot holder. 25.) pin it to your wall like a picture. 26.) send 1 to the david letterman show. 27.) use it to dust your furniture. 28.) send 1 to Michael Jackson to wear as a veil. 29.) insist on wearing it to church. 30.) give it to your wife as an anniversay present. 31.) iron it until the flamingos peel off 32.) lather, rinse, repeat! 33.) use it on your trip for packing breakables. 34.) polish your brass. 35.) give it to a small girl to wear as a dress. 36.) sell it on e-bay and double your money. 37.) wear it on the town to show your moxy. 38.) use it as a bar rag. 39.) wear it one summer and try to return it the next. 40.) makes a great shoe buffer. 41.) tie-dye it and become a phish head or a floydian slipper. 42.) cut if off below your chest and wear it as a belly shirt. 43.) hang it on a pole in your yard to show your allegiance to maggies. 44.) is that a t-shirt in your in your pocket or are you just glad to see me? 45.) put it on the scare crow in your garden. 46.) display it in the alley with other junk and call it art. 47.) makes great nesting material. 48.) use it as a bird cage liner 49.) fly it like a kite. 50.) use it to drain your bacon or tortilla chips. thanks to al & cindy for the t-shirt design. also thanks to louie & sue for their clever "50" ways to use your t-shirt.

Middle: Nancy Erickson, Larry Soulier, Rosa Karl. Above: Lavetta Torke, Don and Lois Albrecht

Nancy Erickson

we again met Nancy. She asked us to help her and the staff sing Happy Birthday to a guy who came all the way from South Dakota. We did and the guy we sang to overheard that it was my wife's birthday that week. He told Nancy and we did it all over again to my very embarrassed wife, Joy.

The Northwoods tour went to Bayfield many more times and on each trip I went to Maggie's, found Nancy (if she was there) and got a picture of Nancy and me for my wife Joy. One last trip, about 2016, Nancy was not there but the bartender remembered me doing that so I got a picture with a "stand in" for Nancy ... the bartender.

I never met Mary Rice but saw her house up on the hill near the Iron Bridge.

Once I was at the tiny bar and two other bikers came in: Robert Plant and Steve Miller. From that day on I told friends "I was at Maggie's and had beers with Steve Miller and Robert Plant." (Steve Miller is from the Steve Miller Band and took lessons from Les Paul. Robert Plant was from Led Zeppelin.) Okay ... not the real guys with those names but it is a fun Maggie's story.

—Thomas and Joy Ristau

BEST SEAT AT THE BAR

I thought I would contribute something to the Maggie's book. I started working Maggie's during my freshman year of high school and continued to work there during the summers through my freshman year of college. I began bussing tables but by the time I was in college, I was usually working behind the bar in some capacity. Working at Maggie's allowed me to meet so many people who I now consider friends, and gave me useful life skills, particularly how to deal with difficult people and tough situations.

However, **my favorite memory** about Maggie's is from a day I had been tending bar. A customer I knew from many years earlier walked in with his friend for a bite to eat. Actually, this customer had asked for a seat at the bar on numerous occasions while I was working. I assumed he just liked eating at the bar to avoid waiting for a table, until he finally asked me out on a date! Thanks to Maggie's, I now have an amazing daughter, Nori, and get to live in Bayfield on a beautiful farm with my partner Josh. Had I not been working at Maggie's, we may have never gone on that first date. I'm grateful for the opportunity and for everything I gained while working for Mary. Warm regards ...

—Esme Martinson, below, with Nori and Josh

2001 mid-winter table

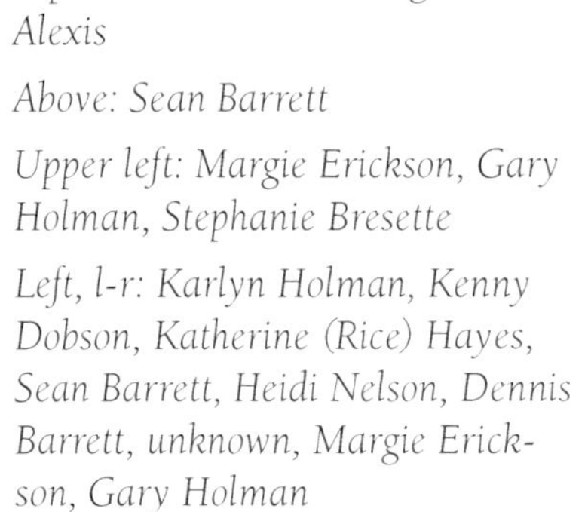

Top: Dan Priebe and daughter Alexis

Above: Sean Barrett

Upper left: Margie Erickson, Gary Holman, Stephanie Bresette

Left, l-r: Karlyn Holman, Kenny Dobson, Katherine (Rice) Hayes, Sean Barrett, Heidi Nelson, Dennis Barrett, unknown, Margie Erickson, Gary Holman

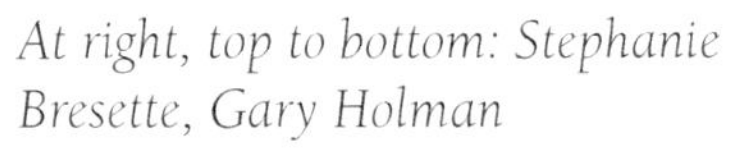

At right, top to bottom: Stephanie Bresette, Gary Holman

The people make it happen

Rosa Karl, Sandy Kuepfer

Dawn Hauser, Kevin Karaba

Randy Anderson, Heather Atherton and fellow Northland College student Andi Macko

Dick Radke

Above: Lois Stensvad, Margie Erickson, Mary Kay Defoe, Brenda Erickson,

Middle left: Ivy Meierotto

Left: Lois Stensvad

the Flamingo Flyer

from MAGGIE'S EMPORIUM

VOLUME 1 Version 83 WINTER 1990

Bristolgate

The story of Bristolgate begins in the fall of '80 just after Mary buys Maggie's. Office space was the last thing on her mind, so when I showed up to count the first days receipts Mary takes me around the corner and stops at the doorway to the bathroom. "Oh Boy!" I'm thinking to myself." Isn't this just about the finest office space a girl could ever want!" As I sit at my desk, a card table that had three and maybe three-quarters legs, I'm thinking, "Things can only get better."

Not too many months later the big move to the upstairs at Maggie's occurred making life a little easier. But with each new business that Mary picked up in the Decade, along came a new piece of office equipment and a person to go with it. Pretty soon it wasn't just me up there anymore. It was me and a desk, Todd and a desk, Molly and a desk and Robin and a desk. All in a space that made us glad we all showered daily!

Which finally brings me to Bristolgate... Now this is what office space was meant to be. Rooms with a view and so much more! If we can just figure out the new phone system we've got it made!

You can reach us at 779-5010, but remember, we'll probably leave you in *Phone Limbo Land* for the first few weeks. Be patient, Mary has complete faith in our ability to conquer the system.

As soon as all the dust has settled we'll be having an open house to celebrate. In the meantime feel free to stop by and say hello. I'd like to say the coffee's always on but we don't have a coffee pot yet. Oh the things to come! Heidi

Adendum: We now have a coffee pot, so bring one of your Norwegian friends with you and we'll put it to the test.

Hello former Maggie-ites ("Mag-pies"),

It's Maggie's 10th Anniversary and we're celebrating!!!!!! Please come and be a part of it all. It's Flamingo Madness week, beginning with a Parade on Sunday August 26th - WE'd LOVE to have you participate - wear old Maggie's T's if you have one - Bring your kids, your dog, your friends from Iowa..... Don't be afraid to be tacky!!!!

Tuesday, the 27th is Jr. Yeska - Remember when day. Come in be a guest cook, waitress, bartender - If you wear old maggie's attire we'll give you a free drink!!!!!!!!

And if you always wanted to be in the Miss America Contest - NOW'S the time - Thursday august 30th at 10pm - Be There - the talent competition will no doubt be unparalleled, not to mention the swimsuit and evening gown events. It's going to be the excitement of the year!!!!! - As Bob Barker always says - " Have your pets spayed or neutered" !!!!!!!!!

On Saturday September 1st, there will be a steak cook-out event in Maggie's parking lot - Don't forget to come.

If you have any stupid questions, nagging doubts, absurd answers or moving suggestions ... call us at 779 - 5010 !!!!!!!!!!!!!!!!!!!!!!!!!

See Ya Soon,
Janel
et al

Bruce Bowers

Mike Boutin at right

OUTSTANDING BAYFIELD CITIZEN

Tips For Tourists

Billy Hauser, outstanding citizen of the quarter, has made an incredible observation and has been kind enough to share it with visitors to the area. Billy says that "when you've been here long enough that it's necessary to do some launder'n, the two machines in the middle just south of the orange ones, hold one third more stuff than all the others." Only after much pondering and extreme fine tuning of his observational skills, (Bates Bar is within easy walking distance of the laundry), was Billy able to make conclusively, with unwavering conviction this statement of irrefutable fact. If that in itself isn't enough to take your breath away and leave you senseless, Billy has agreed to reveal without prodding or remuneration a laundrymat secret with wide spread implications. And I quote, "When it comes to the dry'n part of your launder'n don't put more than a dollar's worth of quarters in there cause that damn machine can't count past four." Now just take a moment to think about that!

From the Ski Hill Kitchen

We had a very busy holiday season and it was great to see those shining winter faces again. The Ski Hill Kitchen has a few new temptations to keep you from getting the slumps on the slopes, like pizza burgers and chicken strips. Most popular by far however, has been our very own homemade pizza. By the way don't forget our, we-can't-make'm-fast-enough-chocolate-chip-cookies. Why we've been told that it's worth the trip to the Ski Hill just to get your hands on one.

Just one last item. Wednesday ski packages include specially prepared meals from our famous "Kitchen". So what are you waiting for? Give us a call. Find out what's cook'in and let's go skiing!

Maggie's 10 Year Anniversary

Greetings from Maggie's, Bayfield's one and only shrine to Pink Flamingos, food and fun. Although it's winter and you must "watch out where the Huskies go," you needn't eat that yellow snow cause we're open daily from 6a.m. to 9p.m. (10p.m. on week-ends) serving great homemade meals. Now suppose you're just a little bit thirsty, well we have that covered, from our bar, the only one in the area with an overhead train, we serve great cocktails, imported and domestic beers, California wines and special hot drinks to take the chill off. You can count on the bar being open late because we consider missing "Cheers" a sacrilege, even though that means struggling through the 'local snooze'.

Throughout the ski season, just hand your Mt. Ashwabay lift ticket to one of our fine bartenders and have a drink on Maggie's. Every Sunday you can cheer on our ice racing team lead by Jim Defoe and his '75' Caddy.

We are spicing up your winter with Ethnic Dinners on Wednesday nights at least once a month, so watch for our special notices with dates and times. Included will be Chinese, Mexican, Northern Italian, Greek and maybe even Indonesian. There's more. Every Tuesday night an All-You-Can-Eat Shrimp Feast and on February 14th our own version of "Cupid's Caper, A Culinary Delight" complete with decorations done in the unique fashion you would expect from Maggie's.

So, cast caution aside, come see us, we're a little looney, but you'll love us and you can even take home a t-shirt or sweat shirt to prove it.

As always your tacky but never tedious friends at Maggie's!

Above left: Todd Kessler, Dave Nixon on the motorcycle
Above right: John Hanson, Jack Gunderson

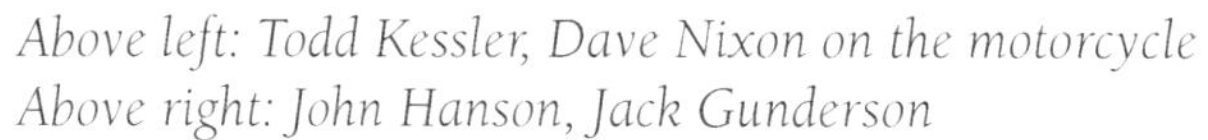

BAYFIELD BUILDING

PERMIT

Permit No. 961

For 5' x 18' Addition

Location Maggie's

Date 3/4/91 By ________
Building Inspector

POST IN
CONSPICUOUS PLACE

PLUMBING	ELECTRICAL	CONSTRUCTION
SEWER ________	TEMP ________	FNDN. ________
R. I. ________	R. I. ________	FRMG. ________
FINAL ________	FINAL ________	FINAL ________

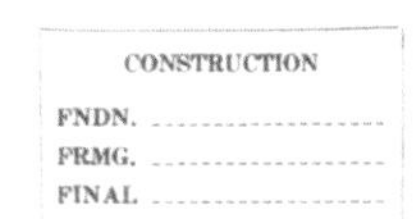

Top left: Marie Brauns. Top right: Dickie Goodlet
Above left: Howie Dietz. Above right: Eleanor Frostman
Below middle: Marion Goodlet. Right: Tom Mitchell

Maggie's 10 Year Anniversary

Left: Ryan Connell

Far left: Kenny Dobson leaning on truck with Linda and Roger Bristol. Jim Frostman in the background.

Below: Heidi Nelson

Ervin Larson

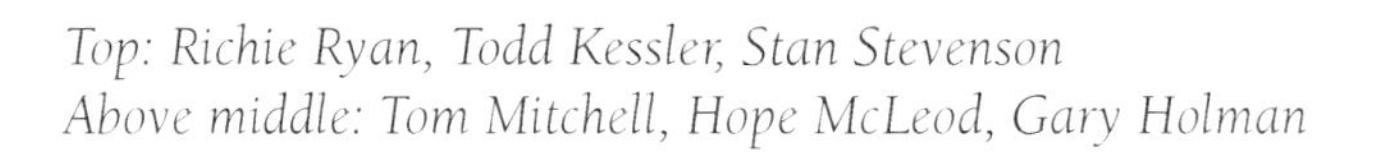

Top: Richie Ryan, Todd Kessler, Stan Stevenson
Above middle: Tom Mitchell, Hope McLeod, Gary Holman

Rosa Karl with baby Gavin Soulier. Brendan Soulier at left, Zack Leal in foreground. Along with their sister Sadie Soulier, they grew up in Maggie's working with their dad, Larry. All four of them worked there as teens and adults.

DRINKING AND TELLING STORIES

On Friday evening, May 15, 1998, the Chequamegon Bay Area was under a tornado warning. My son, Zack Leal, (four at the time), then-boyfriend Larry Soulier, and I lived in a 2nd story Bayfield apartment. I was nine months pregnant with our son Brendan and it was my due date. We decided Maggie's was probably the safest place to go so we headed there. My mom, Gina Karl, was cooking. Larry helped her and other staff get ready in case the winds got more dangerous. Zack and I headed into the basement along with patrons of Maggie's, most holding a fresh drink. The basement was unfinished and spooky, with an unfinished ceiling. I vaguely remember dirt or rough concrete walls in the back corner. We hunkered down until the bartender, Steve Cvek, gave the all clear. The patrons barely glanced at him with no response. They were drinking, telling stories, and having a "hurricane party." Steve said, "Rosa, would you and Zack like to come upstairs?" We followed him and left the others to party! —*Rosa Karl*

Manypenny, August, 1987 photo sent by Marti Peterson, BHA. "I worked as bartender/waitress when Maggie's first opened. Henry Wachsmuth and Cindy Kovachevich were among the staff too. It was crazy busy with a lot of late night closings and good times!"

Larry Soulier, Cindy Andersen, Sam Miller, Katie Poch, Liz Boyd

Ultimate party girl!

NORTHERN NEW YEAR'S SURPRISE

Mary threw a lot of parties, but best of all were her annual "Northern New Year's" celebrations. These were held after the holiday season and gave people a chance to shake off the January doldrums on the third Saturday of the first month of the New Year. One hundred plus invitees jammed into the Knight House ready to party into the wee hours.

Partygoers were instructed to dress up for the occasion and many came in costume or formal wear: men in tuxedos with colorful vests and bow ties, women in slinky dresses and gowns, some with wigs and exaggerated makeup. It was a mix of New Years Eve, Mardi Gras and Rio Carnival and people let their hair down in more ways than one.

The evening started with drinks served from a bar in the garage. Guests mingled throughout the Knight House and Carriage House. About an hour into the evening, Mary rang a bell and ordered us to gather for entertainment by a mystery guest who had been hidden in the upper floor and made an entrance down the grand staircase to where we gathered. It was a highlight of the evening and everyone was buzzing with anticipation.

Suddenly a familiar voice began singing upstairs. I don't remember the song, but it may have been "Sweet Caroline" or "Holy, Holy." We were amazed, Mary had hired Neil Diamond! We couldn't believe it! Of course, nothing was impossible once Mary decided to do something.

All eyes were on the staircase as a figure, still singing, came into view. But instead of Neil Diamond, it was a handsome young black man who, if you closed your eyes, sounded exactly like Neil Diamond. We were astounded and looked at each other in disbelief. Mary had sprung the ultimate surprise on us: "Black Diamond," aka Theron Denson from Nashville, who we learned later had built his career as the world's only African-American Neil Diamond tribute entertainer. We still couldn't believe our eyes.

Black Diamond took his place in the spotlight, turned on his backup music and sang a string of Neil Diamond hits. He had a great voice and Diamond's singing style down perfectly. It was indeed a night to remember, one of many Mary gave us over the years.

—John Hanson (below with Mary)

Mary and longtime friend John Hanson

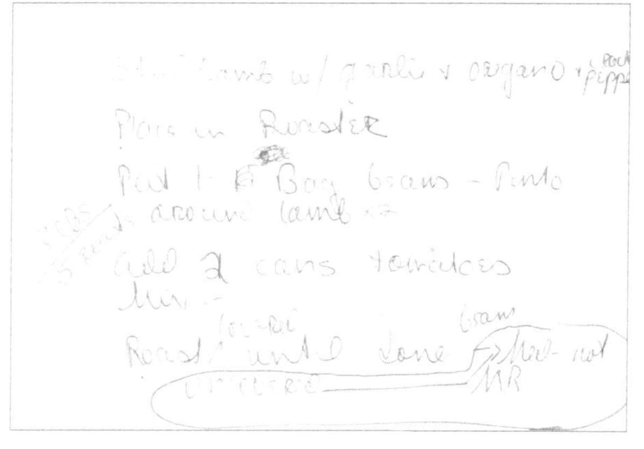

Maggie's Cup Race

Maggie's Cup started in the early '80s and continued until 2019. T-shirts went to the first place boat and their crew. It was "epic" if you won a Maggie's Cup t-shirt. Mary also sponsored the A.D. Bill Hulings Cup in 2012 in honor of her father. Maggie's Cup was a buoy race and the Hulings Cup race is around Madeline Island over Labor Day weekend.

WINNING SAILBOAT RACE

In 1987, some sailboat racers from Bayfield convinced us to participate in the Bayfield Race Week sailing event. Problem was, we were from Sturgeon Bay, Wisconsin. We sailed across Lake Michigan, up the St. Mary's River, through the locks, and transited the length of Lake Superior to get our boat there! But it was worth the effort for all the fun and camaraderie, especially at Maggie's, after the races.

One of the races was the Maggie's Cup Race, in which we won First Place: a beautiful pottery trophy, flamingos and all!

Later in the 1990s we taught sailing in Bayfield, and Maggie's was again our special place. Lots of fond memories. But we never met Mary Rice until we sailed to Hope Town in the Bahamas. Finally we were able to put together the person with the sponsorship of the Maggie's Cup, from a couple of decades earlier!

—Sue and George Holloway

Above left: The A.D. Bill Hulings Cup. Above right: Charlie Erickson, a boater who owned Quintessence. *At right: Sailboat* Angisina *owned by Andy Spence-Parsons*

CRUISING AND RACING

I've been a cruising and racing sailor in the Apostles for over 50 years. "Legacy" comes to mind as we remember this generous Bayfield benefactor who provided great food. Please honor her by keeping fast food and chains out of Bayfield and model your life to be a legacy such as Mary's. *—Leroy Horn*

Below: Sailboat Chase, *owned by Charlie Schroeder was first place Hulings Cup in 2013 and first place winner again in 2017. He is pictured here, to Mary's left, holding the trophy.*

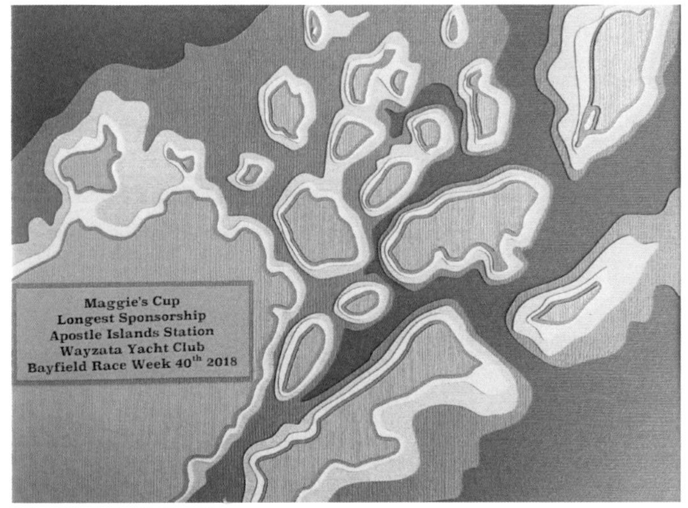

Maggie's Cup Trophy that AIS gave Mary for the longest sponsorship. Bayfield Race Week 40th year

Zig Zag owner Jim Vaudreuil won the 2012 Maggie's Cup. *Below: Maggie's Cup previous winners*

Above and below: Maggie's Cup previous winners and friends

The people make it happen

Above: Irene and Chad Defoe

Below: Fritz Hauser

Above: Denise Koch

Below, at right, and at lower right: Hayley Webster

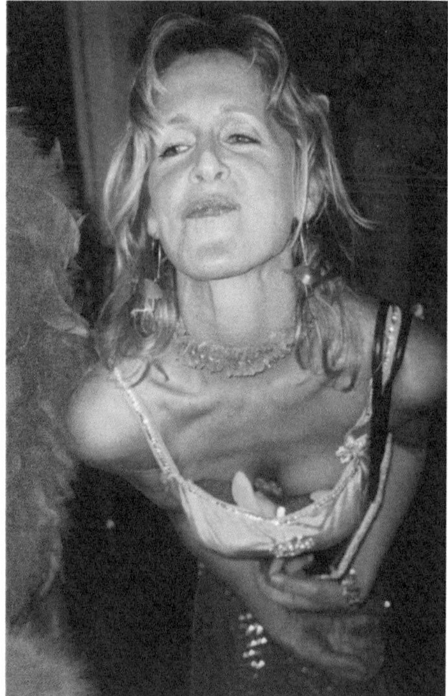

Andy Falconer

Hayley Webster

Jack Gunderson and Mary

Top: Molly Rice
Middle: Karen Soderman
Above: Tom Mitchell and Pat Juett's daughter, Oona Mitchell

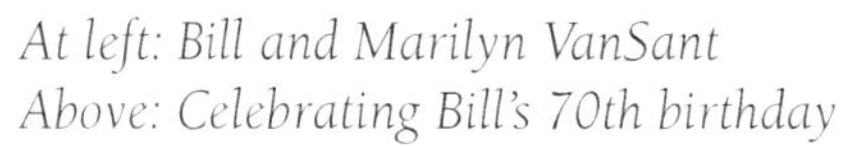

At left: Bill and Marilyn VanSant
Above: Celebrating Bill's 70th birthday

Lloyd Turner

Above, l-r: long-term employees Irene Radke, Karmyn Simmons, Mary Kay Defoe, and Nancy Erickson at the 25th Anniversary parade

Below: Kaite Sweval, known as Kitten on her guest checks

WHAT BAYFIELD USED TO BE LIKE

It was a very hot steamy summer night in Bayfield about 10 years ago—very muggy and nightfall had not cooled it off, unusual being so close to the big Lake Superior.

Carl French, an old friend of mine and Mary's was visiting from the Philippines, where he had been selling yachts. He and I had been riding *all over town* that hot afternoon in my 1967 Cutlass Oldsmobile convertible while one of us squirted a "super soaker" (huge squirt gun) at people we deemed squirtable, and even those we deemed not squirtable! We spotted Chris Pederson in front of Xanadu who was an easy target! Normally "crabby," we thought he was not squirtable, but it was sweltering, and he laughed and loved it! WOW. The water range was 30-some feet!

We were having a riot.

After stopping for dinner at Greunke's, we calmed down and decided to head for home, near the Apostle Highlands Golf Course. So, top still down on the convertible, still a sultry night, **we slowly rode by Maggie's** and I said, "Lets peek in the window and see what's going on."

Sure enough, Mary was holding court with 8-10 dinner guests right up in the front of Maggie's at the first big table. I said, "Carl, let's crash!" We went to the front door and found it locked. The waitress saw us and said, "Sorry, we're closed to which I said, "I have to tell Mary something important." Because the waitress knew me, she let us in! We came in all innocently cheerful and, of course, we had our super soaker!

I start squirting Mary right away. All the guests are aghast! They didn't know what to think. Then Mary let out this loud, boisterous laugh, and shouted, "**This is what Bayfield used to be like!**" We could see her guests breathing sighs of relief and they started laughing too.Then Mary's pal Kenny jumped up, got on the floor and with Carl riding him like a pony I super soaked both of them. Everybody was shrieking with laughter, especially Mary, who loved every minute!

We packed our water gun and sweetly bid adieu!

—Judith Lokken-Strom, owner of Gruenke's 1st Street Inn in Bayfield

Above: Mary Rice at home, party time.
Below: Jim Erickson, Heidi Nelson

Top left: Jim Webster Top middle: John Hanson. Top right: Al Radley, Sue Glover. Far left: Guess who!? Left: Pam Pratt. Near left: Irene Defoe. Above: Mary and grand-daughter Sevona

The people make it happen

Above: Janet Sternat. Below: Steve Saetre

Above: Steve Soderman and Bob Adams. Below: John and Libby Telford. Below: Nicole Frechette, Diane Brander

Above: Ruthie Moon and Mary
Below: Lu Eckels

The people make it happen

John Hanson

Above: John Murphy, Joyce Howe, John Rice.
Below: Rex and Peg Dollinger

Working at Maggie's

Above: Heidi Nelson. Below: Sue Glover

Top: Larry Soulier, Kevin Caroba. Above: Irene Radke
Below: Karmyn Simmon

The people make it happen

FIRST BLUE MOON BALL

The very first Blue Moon Ball was held at Maggie's. It was called a "prom for adults." I believe Bob and Diane Brander were crowned King and Queen. I'm scratching my head to think of someone who could confirm this. Everyone that comes to mind though is already dead. But I am 99% sure I'm correct.

—Lloyd Scott Turner

THING THAT ALWAYS GOT ME …

… was that the kitchen staff could tell Mary was in the building before we were told, just by the smell of her perfume.

More than once, a staff member had to go out front and stare down a bad customer, most times for bothering a female waitress.

Every female that ever worked at Maggie's was asked, "Are you Maggie?" Dancing on the pool table was quite the thing back in the day. Once, my husband and brother-in-law got on the pool table with Mary. When the song was over, she could not get down. It took five guys but the laughter that came from her was more fun than any dancing that has ever been done on the pool table. She always had such a good sense of humor about herself.

Mary surprised me for both my 60th birthday and my 65th birthday and I was "just a dishwasher."

So many stories of hauntings: little girl sightings; man in black; mops and brooms coming off the wall aimed at one of the employees; water coming off and on continuously. But it was all part of Maggie's. I certainly enjoyed working there for 14 years. I worked with the same people in the kitchen probably five days a week that whole time and they became one big family. I will always miss our togetherness and we will always be friends

—Cindy Andersen

WHAT CAME FIRST

I believe you are correct, Lloyd. Juniors, then two years as Fisherman's Cove, then it became Maggie's, about 1980. Bob and Diane were in the Virgin Islands by 1982. We called Maggie's during the Blue Moon Ball that we were missing. There was 100 degrees temperature difference between Bayfield and the Virgin Islands.

—Phil Peterson

Maggie's

257 Manypenny
Bayfield, Wi.
715-779-5641

aggies Breakfast
6:00 a.m. to 11:00 a.m.

cial 2 eggs, ...browns or American fries, toast and jelly 4.50
l 3 buckwheats. ...n 4.00
os Flour tortilla, refried beans, ...sauce, sour cream 3.50

Omelettes
Include toast and jelly

.... 2.75 3 egg cheese 3.25
l Ham and cheese, your choice of green peppers, tomato, sour cream 4.75

...rte

.... .60
.... 1.20
.... .95
.... 1.95
...ese 1.20
...l roll .... .95
.... 1.05
...the day .... .95
.... 1.70
.... 1.45

Ala Carte

French toast (3) 1.95
French toast (2) 1.70
Pattie or Link Sausage/Bacon 1.45
Ham 1.70
Hash browns/ American fries 1.20
1/2 grapefruit 1.20
Cantaloupe (in season) 1.70
Yogurt 1.00
Peanut butter .... .60
Jack Gunderson's maple syrup .... .60
Fruit compote 1.75
Slice of Cheese .... .25-.50
(Swiss, Colby or Cheddar)

...ges

Coffee .... .60
Decaffeinated .... .75
Tea .... .50
Iced tea .... .50
Flavored tea .... .60
Cocoa .... .60
Milk .... .65 & 1.15
Orange juice .... 1.25 & 1.95
Grapefruit juice .... 1.25 & 1.95
Grape juice .... 1.25 & 1.95
Pineapple juice .... 1.25 & 1.95
Tomato juice .... 1.25 & 1.95
Apple juice .... 1.25 & 1.95

Biscuit Menu

Biscuit and butter .... .60
Biscuit and butter, cheese .... .85
Add On:
Tomato, onion or lettuce .... .35
Egg or turkey .... .60
Pattie Sausage or Canadian bacon .... .80

Did you know...
We make our own jams and jellies made with local fruits and that they're especially good on our homemade breads, buns and muffins! Rob said so!!
Check the blackboard for the features of the morn.
Substitutions .75 extra No 1/2 orders please

United Sta...
Budweiser
Budweiser
Coors
Coors Ligh...
Leinenkug...
Miller
Miller Gen...
Miller Lite
Old Milwa...
Old Style
Old Style L...
Pabst
Stroh's

Premiums
Andeker
Augsberge...
Augsberge...
Michelob
Michelob Light
Special Export

On Tap
Augsberger Light 55-.75
Hacker Pschorr 90-1.50-2.00
Pitcher Augsberger 4.00
Pitcher Hacker Pschorr 8.00

Non Alcoholic
Kingsbury 1.10
Moussy 2.00

Pop and Mineral Water
Coke 35-.40-.75
Diet Coke 35-.40-.75
Sprite 35-.40-.75
Tonic 35-.40-.75
Club Soda 35-.40-.75
LaCroix 1.00

Coffee, Tea and Juices
Apple Juice 1.25-1.95
Tomato Juice 1.25-1.95
Orange Juice 1.25-1.95

Dinkel Acker 2.50
Hacker Pschorr Weiss 3.00
St. Pauli Light 2.25
St. Pauli Dark 2.25

Holland
Amstel Light 2.50
Grolsch 16oz. 3.00
Heineken 2.25

Ireland
Guiness Stout 2.50
Harp Lager 2.50

Mexico
Corona Extra 2.25
Dos Equis 2.00
Cervesa Negra Modelo 2.50

Norway
Ringnes 2.50

Wines
Bartles & Jaymes Wine Cooler 2.00
Riunite Lambrusco 1.50

Maggie's Dinner

Appetizers

French Fries **1.00**
German Fries **1.00**
Homemade Chips **1.00**
Classic Chips **1.00**
Onion Rings **2.00**
Whitefish Livers as available .. **2.50**
Chicken Wings **1.25**
(Sweet & Sour or Barbeque 1.50)

Maggie's International Burgers

USA East **2.50**
Hamburger, french fries, pickle.
With cheese .25 extra.
Bleu Cheese .50 extra.

Canadian Burger **4.00**
Canadian bacon, swiss cheese on a beef pattie, french fries.

Mexican Burger **3.75**
Cheese and refried beans on a beef pattie, topped with hot sauce and sour cream, taco chips.

CIA Burger **4.00**
Swiss, colby, bleu cheese or cheddar cheese, a beef pattie, french fries.

Italian Burger **3.75**
Pizza sauce, pepperoni, mozzarella cheese on a beef pattie, homemade chips.

French Burger **3.75**
Mushrooms, red onion and blue cheese on a beef pattie, french fries.

USA West **4.00**
California burger, french fries, pickle.
With cheese .25 extra.
Bleu Cheese .50 extra.

German Burger **3.75**
Homemade sauerkraut on a beef pattie, pickle, German fries.

Greek Burger **3.75**
Marinated black olives, onion, cherry tomatoes, feta cheese on a beef pattie, served on pita bread.

Irish Burger **4.25**
Corned beef, cheddar cheese and horseradish sauce on a beef pattie, sauce, classic chips.

Danish Burger **4.00**
Shredded pot roast in beer, horseradish sauce, classic chips, pickle.

English Burger **4.00**
Fresh Lake Superior whitefish or trout, deep fried, on a bun, homemade chips.

Burgers

Hamburger **2.50**
Cheeseburger **2.75**
California Burger **3.00**
California Cheeseburger **3.25**
(All burgers served with potato chips, pickle)

Salads

Tossed Garden Salad **1.25**
Maggie's Chef Salad **4.00**
Italian Vegetable Salad **2.00**
Greek Salad **3.50**
Fruit Salad **4.00**
(Honey Celery Seed Dressing)
Pasta Salad **4.50**
(Changes daily)

Italian or French dressing included.
1000 Island .50 Bleu Cheese .75
Creamy Cucumber .75

Maggie's Fresh Deep Fried Lake Superior Whitefish or Trout .. **7.50**
Served with a tossed or Italian salad, baked or french fried potatoes, roll and butter.

Maggie's Fresh Bayfield Poached Whitefish or Lake Trout **7.50**
Served with a tossed or Italian salad, baked or french fried potatoes, roll and butter.

Top Butt Steak Sandwich **6.95**
6 oz. top butt served with a tossed salad, baked or french fried potatoes, roll and butter.

...remember what we said about lunch? It's the same for dinner plus we also whip up our own dressings for our light and lovely salads!

Substitutions .75 extra No 1/2 orders please

A SHIMMERING EVENING

There were so many great dinners at Maggie's: with family, with friends, and even solo. They were unfailingly, reliably good: tasty, accompanied by a glass of good wine, a yummy piece of pie, and most often, a visit with someone we hadn't seen for awhile. The one that stands out, though, was the first time Jeff and I got together for dinner with Mom.

It was in the fall, a chilly, clear night. We had a great time chatting and visiting. About 8:00 p.m. it was time to leave and we stepped into the dark night. And looked up. There, far above us, was the most spectacular aurora borealis I have ever seen. It filled the sky with pulsing, white and green cascades of light. Somehow, behind those, were the brightly shimmering stars of the Milky Way. We were transfixed with delight and awe and watched for at least 20 minutes.

If not for dinner at Maggie's, we would have missed it completely. I've not seen anything like it since.

—Kristy Jensch (at left with Jeff Silbert)

THAT POOL TABLE AGAIN … !

It was the early '80s on one of those nights, after the kitchen closed, when Maggie's transformed into a mecca for hedonists. Kenny Dobson had made a plywood cover for the pool table so we could crowd together up there and dance to the jukebox. My story happened on top of that pool table the night that Maggie's sponsored the Ms. America Pageant complete with talent, gown, and swimsuit competitions.

Local hedonists accepted the challenge and we costumed up to impress the judges with our beauty and amazing talents displayed on that infamous plywood stage. My sash read "Ms. Ice Road" and my gown was one of Mary's satin nightgowns, accented by a white rubber swim cap strapped under my chin. Although my purple swimsuit and stuffed matching tights (stick-out butt and big lumpy legs) was a vision, I'm certain it was my Gilda Radner walk that earned me points. I remember Mary howling with laughter and egging me on. With the crowd warmed up and boozie, like we were, it was time for the talent contest. When it was my turn, I sat cross-legged with a small tray in my lap and confidently hand rolled cigarettes which I tossed to the crowd.

The judges tallied the scores and Mary announced the first runner up: Lake Superior Sturgeon (Kenny Dobson). Then she placed the crown on top of Ms Ice Road's lucky swim cap and **I became the first and only Maggie's Ms. America**: another story officially added to thousands of others about Mary to whom we lovingly lift a glass in her honor.

—Deb Weber

10-17-06

...them it may concern...
We are regular Maggie's...

Kind thoughtful and pleasant they all were to various customers and their individual needs. One table requested extra tortilla's for their fajita's — and it was done with a cheerful "of course" — An elderly couple came in wanting fish — they (the waitresses) explained that Maggie's didn't have any that day and were helpful in directing them to someplace that might have it — All were so "kind" to everyone — How Nice!! Linda

Madison April 26 2005

Flamingos on Bascom Hill

Early one morning in 1979, the University and the city of Madison woke up to the spectacular sight of thousands of pink flamingo ornaments filling the lawns of Bascom Hill on the U.W. Madison campus. The student government "officials" from the Pail & Shovel party, also responsible for Madison's ephemeral replica of the Statue of Liberty on frozen lake Mendota, had looted, and some say squandered, student government funds to create the awesome display. Now most reasonable people agreed that the money was well spent.

Hi Brenda & Irene! Willemijn and Jikke here! We safely arrived in Madison again, and from here we'd like to thank you both again for the great time we had in Bayfield, in Maggie's and in the Bayfield Inn. We're wearing our t-shirts and keep very good memories on the time we spent with you! Please send us a mail-address, so we can send you our pictures! Hope to see you again! Jikke & Willemijn Bye!

Maggie's (Brenda & Irene)
257 Manypenny Avenue
Bayfield WI 54814

41 Photo © Michael Kienitz

The Flamingos of Bascom Hill

From a party who thinks you could use a few more flamingos.

Post Card

Maggie's
257 W. Manypenny Ave
Bayfield Wi.
54814

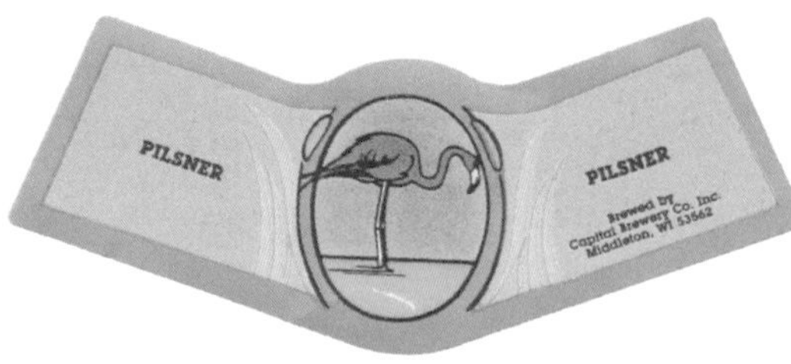
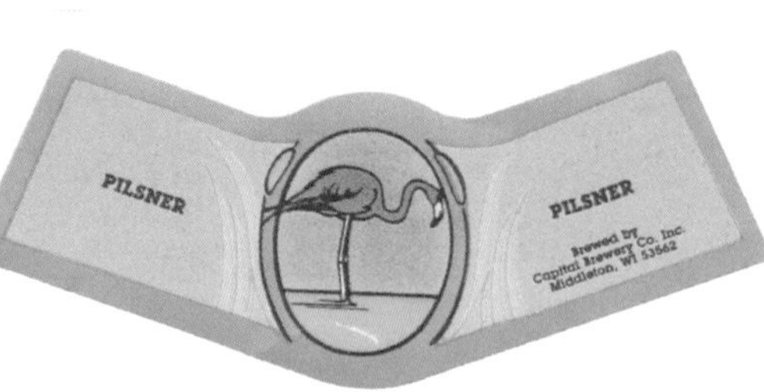

Postcard notes of thanks; anonymous postcard recommending more flamingos; bumper sticker; 20th Anniversary sticker; gift card; temporary tattoo "Celebrating 20 Years"; another sticker! and Maggie's Pilsner label

6 Sept.

Dear Margie,

We want to thank you for your wonderful generosity. We've enclosed a couple of pictures of Dana enjoying her handmade blanket— on the floor, just as you suggested. She loves playing, kicking and cooing.

We enjoyed our visit to Bayfield. The abundant hospitality extended by Mary and all of you is so appreciated. We felt so welcomed and cared for.

Warmly,

Mari, Len &

Above: Chelsea Nelson

Maggie's once had its own Pilsner brew. It was created by Capital Brewery out of Madison, WI and run through a northern distributor.

Forty years before its 2020 closing, Maggie's opened its pink (well, turquoise) door.

Matches, pens, playing cards, pencils, magnets, stickers, and wooden nickels. Was there nothing that Mary didn't put the logo on?

Below: Taken to task!

The #1 Most Significant Event Of 1980

Maggie's Opens Her Doors & The Legend Begins

(I told my waitress to show all employees)

Dear Owner, give us a break, you can't afford air conditioning?? It's bad enough for customers. We feel sorry for your employees!!

Rick + Viktoriya Hopperstad
Schooner Bay, Marina summer residents

The people make it happen

NEW OWNER

Tom and I loved Maggie's and went there all the time. I remember a trip to Bayfield to investigate the area as a possible place to live, just about the time Maggie's opened for business in 1980. We drove into town looking for a place to eat. Tom had been to Bayfield several times in the past, visiting his friend, Jan Moran. He remembered a little corner bar and suggested we "just go there for a hamburger and a beer." I think the bar was Juniors. Anyway, I had heard about The Rittenhouse and I thought that since we had driven all the way to Bayfield, we could at least try and find a really nice restaurant. After all, we could get a beer and a burger anywhere!

Terri Wagner, Tom Kvanbeck

We drove by Maggie's initially and went back when Tom suggested we try it because it looked like there was a new owner. **It immediately became our favorite restaurant where we took everyone who came to visit us once we moved to Washburn**. I think our three kids may have set the record for number of Flamingo Tenders eaten by a single family unit. Talk about an institution in Bayfield. Bet there are some pretty wild stories …

—*Terri Wagner*

REVENGE!

It was a gottcha moment! In the early years, there was an old, fairly large naked doll that would randomly show up in the weirdest spots in an attempt to scare the unsuspecting. One day, Ken Dobson *(photos at left)* placed it inside the chest freezer that was behind the bar and in front of the walk-in cooler. Mary found it first and of course plotted her revenge. **Within a few days, she lucked out when the health inspector walked in**. She immediately knew how to get back at Ken and asked the inspector if he would kindly write us up for a violation of health standards and fine us $300. Fortunately, he had a sense of humor and supplied her with the bogus paperwork.

Upon presenting Ken with the paperwork, his face went white while the rest of us were trying our hardest not to break into laughter. He immediately took off out to his truck, grabbed his checkbook, came back inside, and wrote a $300 check to Mary so fast it made our heads spin! I don't remember how long she hung onto it before she told Ken the truth but the health inspector got a laugh out of it every time he came back!

—*Heidi Nelson*

Karlyn and Gary Holman of Washburn (upper left), Wisconsin often found themselves seated at Mary's table at Maggie's.

Karlyn (left) and Mary bonded over their love of painting and traveled worldwide with other artists on Karlyn's watercolor workshops. Mary and Karlyn were both generous and creative women who loved their communities, and both shared a mischievous nature which led to many fun-filled adventures and over-the-top social events. And Gary, the unofficial poet laureate of Washburn, was always along to commemorate the events in limerick form (at right).

—Terri Wagner

SUNG TO "IT'S A GRAND OLD NAME"

Oh it's Maggie's, Maggie's, a city slicker's dream come true … The help is kind of queer, there's import beer and the food's not bad …
Oh it's Maggie's, Maggie's, the train runs when the barkeep says … You have to stand in line but that is fine, it's a grand old place …
Oh it's Maggie's, Maggie's, the joint's been here for just ten years … Yes it was Mary's dream, a wild ass scheme, to serve fine food …
Oh it's Maggie's, Maggie's, an old paymaster's booth we're told … It was first Juniors bar by the railroad cars, now it's Maggie's dream.

—Gary Holman, 1990

Construction, 1999

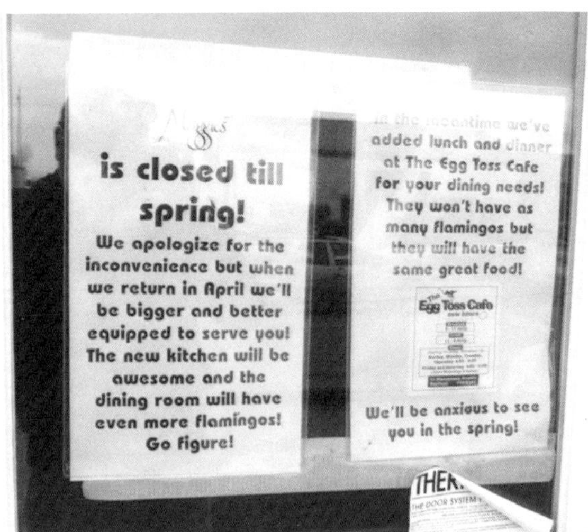

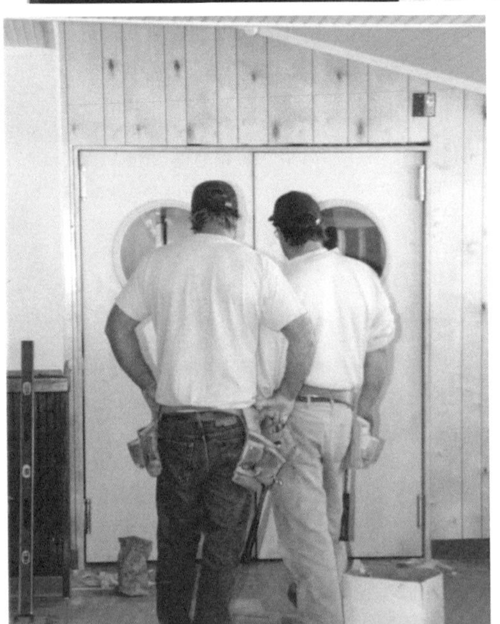

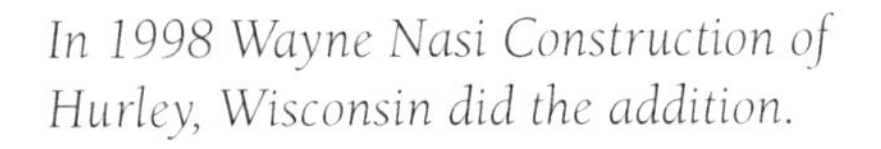

In 1998 Wayne Nasi Construction of Hurley, Wisconsin did the addition.

Rich Wszalek of One Guy Plumbing

Miller
HIGH LIFE
John Erickson Fisheries
FRESH SMOKED
OGAARD'S
FISHERIES
FRESH AND SMOKED
Budweiser
AVAILABLE COLD

Tyvek

Budweiser

TOM LAZORIK
ELECTRIC
800-555-5949
WAYNE NASI
CONST. INC.
DURO-LAST ROOFING
ONE GUY & SONS
Plumbing & Heating
BAYFIELD, WI 779-5081
Superior
Drywall & Paint, Inc.

Re-opening, 1999

Far left: Andy (Brown) Falconer and Charlie Brown

Middle: Kelly Haskins in the kitchen

Above, top: Lois Stensvad

Above: Erin English and Brenda Erickson

Re-opening, 1999

Re-opening, 1999

Far left top: Kenny Dobson, Rich Wszalek

Far left middle: Kenny Dobson, Rich Wszalek, Pat Juett, Margie Erickson, Debbie Lind

Far left bottom at table: Jill Lorenz, Rich Wszalek, Andy (Brown) Falconer, Rudd Falconer, Linda Rise, Andy Noyes

Middle top: Leland LaPointe, Larry Soulier, and Dale Hanson in kitchen

Middle bottom: Linda and Roger Bristol

Above, top: Mary Kay Defoe and Nancy Erickson at computers. Margie Erickson

Above, middle: Dale Hanson, Larry Soulier

At left: Dale Hanson

Re-opening, 1999

Sue Glover, Brenda Erickson

Ed (Edwin Martin) Erickson (1910-2001) was Mayor of Bayfield from 1970 to 1976, and again from 1980 to 1983 and was the force behind lutefisk dinners.

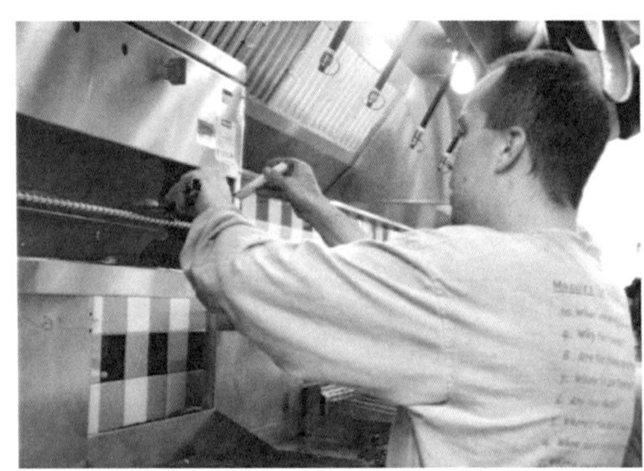

Larry Soulier

Left middle: Charlie Brown, Pat Juett, Margie Erickson, Debbie Lind , Kenny Dobson, Andy (Brown) Falconer
Left, bottom: Lois Stensvad, Nancy Erickson
Above top: Kenny Dobson
Above middle: Charlie Brown, Janet Bewley, Eyleen Burnside, David Saetre

2001

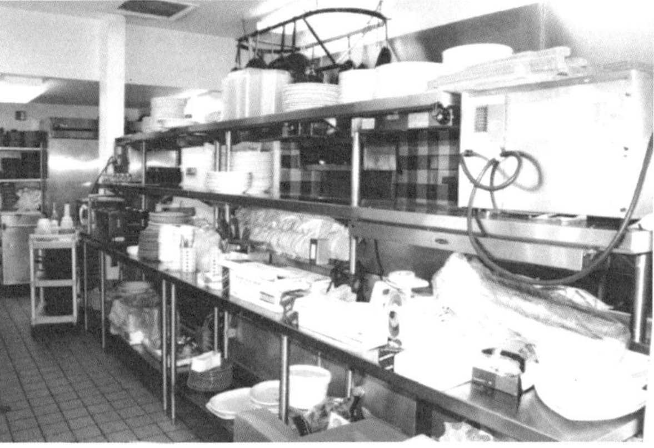

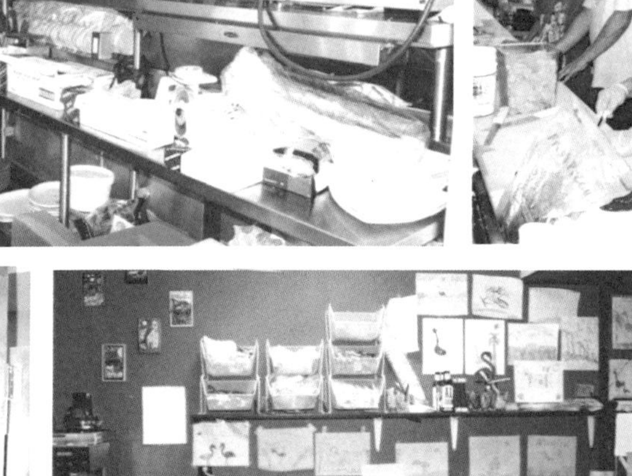

20th anniversary and parade, 2000

Top: "Mumsie"—Kenny Dobson mom

Middle: Mary Kay Defoe, Nancy Erickson

Below: Gina Karl

Below: Irene Defoe

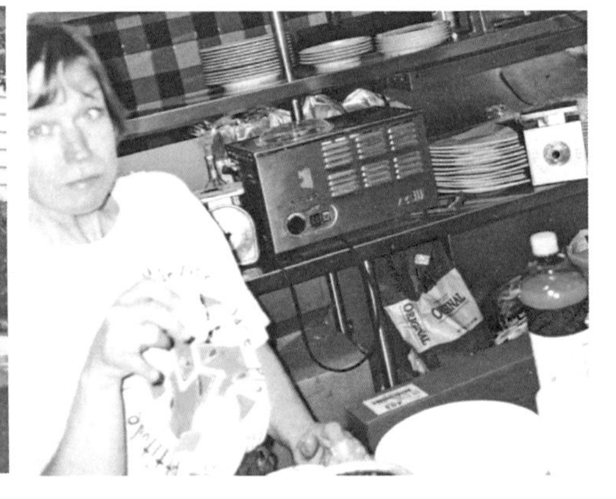

20th anniversary and parade, 2000

Upper right: Stephanie Bresette
Lower right: Timothy Burnside
Below: Dale Hanson, Larry Soulier

20th anniversary and parade, 2000

Top: Nori Perrine, Tony Bruneau, Sue Glover
Left: Irene Defoe. Above: Mary Rice
Below: Ed Erickson and Frank Utpadel

Top: Timothy Burnside, Above: Nancy Erickson
Below, l-r: Burt Faragher, Jerry Dunn, unknown, Gary Holman

20th anniversary and parade, 2000

Top left: Mary greeting friend from the bathtub
Left: Nancy Erickson, Heidi Nelson
Above: Mayor Larry McDonald
Below left: Dewey Bohnert, Lawrence Gordon
Below: Kristy Doman a daughter Kria
Right: Irene Defoe

Above: Randy Anderson, Lois Stensvad

Below: Timothy Burnside

20th anniversary and parade

Denise Koch

Above: Heidi Nelson and Kenny Dobson. Below: Mayor McDonald, Irene Defoe, Stephanie Bresette, Karlyn Holman

Below Lloyd Turner and Denise Koch in the driver's seat

Mayor McDonald, Kenny Dobson

20th anniversary and parade

Above: Mary, Queen of Bayfield
Lower left: Jack Gunderson
Below: Ed Erickson

Above, l-r: Gina Karl, Mary Kay Defoe, Nancy Erickosn, Timothy Burnside. Below: Molly Rice and Blackjack. Bottom: Krista DeFoe, Sonya Henri

Backstage

Governor meets the Queen

Mary with Tommy Thompson, Governor of Wisconsin. Thompson is the longest-serving governor in Wisconsin history, holding office from January 1987 until February 2001, and is the only person to be elected four times.

Clamshells and compliments

BIRTH OF THE FLAMINGO

I can offer you a piece of Maggie's history. I made the sculpture, "Birth of The Flamingo" in May of 2005. Mary commissioned me to make her a weather vane sculpture to be placed on Maggie's roof and this is what I came up with (above). If Botticelli did "Birth of Venus" then surely there was room for another clam shell. Also, while at her Rasina home Mary was going to make a trip to the Uffizi Gallery in Florence where the Botticelli hangs. The winter before Mary left for Italy she mentioned that her staff would secure the necessary permits to install the sculpture on the roof above the entrance. In May, I hired Kenny Dobson to come with his crane to lift it up. All went well until the City of Bayfield came by that afternoon with a cease and desist order for its removal; no permits had been applied for. Four days later, I hired Kenny again but this time to remove it. At least during those few days it showed Bayfield which way the wind blew.

—*Bob Adams*

A REMEMBERED COMPLIMENT

While waiting outside. I met a family with children and grandchildren on the trip. One gal Anna (at left, near the Bayfield Ferry Landing) took a liking to me. While waiting, I overheard young Anna say to her mom, "One day I am going to marry Tom." What a nice compliment from a young gal who I hope I made a good impression on. I was already married! but "teared up" from a great compliment. I hope Anna reads this and has found a nice guy to marry. —*Thomas Ristau*

Denise Koch in Bob Adams' sculpture

More fun at Maggie's

Above: *Lois Stensvad*

Below: *Mary and Larry Soulier*

Pam and Donnie Pratt

Sandy and Butch Kuepfer

Larry Soulier, Rosa Karl

BEER

ASK YOUR WAITRON WHAT'S ON TAP!

MICROBREWERY BEERS

Anchor Steam....................3.75
Bell's Amber....................3.50
Blue Moon Belgian White Ale....................3.50
Gray's Black and Tan....................3.50
Summit Pale Ale, or India Pale....................3.50
Sierra Nevada Pale Ale....................3.50
J.W. Dundee Honey Brown Ale....................3.50

LOCAL BREWS

Lake Superior Brewing Co. Special Ale........ 3.50
South Shore Nut Brown Ale....................3.75

DOMESTIC BEERS

Cans of Budweiser, Bud Light, Miller, Miller Genuine Draft, Miller Lite........ 2.25
Bottles of Leinenkugel and various brews.. 2.50
Michelob....................2.50
Rolling Rock....................2.50
Killian's Red Ale....................2.50
Huber and Huber Bock, cheap, but good 1.75

IMPORTED BEERS

Labatt's Blue *Canada*....................3.50
Pilsner Urquel *Czech Republic*....................4.00
Bass Ale *England*....................3.50
Heineken *Holland*....................3.50
Hacker Pschorr Weiss - 16 ounce *Germany*..... 5.50
Grolsch - 16 ounce *Holland*....................5.50
Guiness Stout *Ireland*....................3.50
Corona *México*....................3.50
Pacifico *Mexico*....................3.50

NON-ALCOHOLIC BEERS

O'Doul's....................2.50
Kalibur....................3.25

POP AND MINERAL WATER

Coke, Diet Coke, Sprite, Club Soda, Ginger Ale, Fresca.....1.50
Sprecher Root Beer....................1.95
Buddy's Orange & Grape....................1.75
Gray's Cream Soda....................1.75
LaCroix Mineral Water....................1.25

OTHER BEVERAGES

Granado Coffee....................1.25
Cocoa....................1.25
Tea, Regular or Herb....................1.25
Large thermos of coffee (to go)........3.75

the egg toss
BAKERY CAFÉ

WINE

WINES BY THE GLASS

2001 Beringer White Zinfandel 3.75
2000 Washington Hills Late Harvest Riesling 5.00
2000 Fetzer Gewurztraminer 4.50
2000 Lagaria Pinot Grigio.........................4.75
2001 Geyser Peak Sauvignon Blanc........5.00
2000 Bulletin Place Chardonnay *Australia*..4.75
1999 Beringer Pinot Noir *Founder's*........5.00
1999 Domaine De L Enclos Cotes du Rhone....4.50
1998 Shale Ridge Merlot 4.75
1999 Cline Zinfandel 5.00
2000 Santa Rita Cabernet Sauvignon *Chile* 4.75
2000 Bogle Petite Sirah 5.25
2000 Fat Bastard Shiraz *France*..............4.75
NV Ramos Pinto L. B. Vintage Port.6.00

WHITE WINES BY THE BOTTLE

2001 Beringer White Zinfandel 15.00
2000 Washington Hills Late Harvest Riesling. 20.00
2000 Fetzer Gewurztraminer 18.00
2000 Napa Wine Company Sauvignon Blanc.... 29.00
2001 Geyser Peak Sauvignon Blanc.......20.00
1999 Domaines DeCoussergues Sauv Blanc 17.00
2001 Giovello Pinot Grigio *Italy* 19.00
2000 Lagaria Pinot Grigio........................17.00
1999 Wild Horse Pinot Blanc...................28.00
1997 Buckeley's Chardonnay 17.00
1998 Lockwood Chardonnay *Estate*.........19.00
1999 Columbia Crest Chardonnay 19.00
2000 Bulletin Place Chardonnay *Australia* 20.00
NV Domaine Ste Michelle Cuvee Brut........ 20.00

Maggie's also offers champagne splits/ask your waitron

RED WINES BY THE BOTTLE

1999 Domaine De L Enclos *Cotes du Rhone*...17.00
1998 Columbia Crest Merlot....................23.00
1998 Shale Ridge Merlot 17.00
1998 LinCourt Pinot Noir *Santa Barbara*...29.00
1999 Benton Lane Pinot Noir 29.00
1999 Wild Horse Pinot Noir 35.00
1999 Beringer Pinot Noir *Founder's*.......20.00
1999 DeLoach Pinot Noir *O.F.S.* 58.00
1999 Cline Zinfandel 20.00
1998 Deux Amis Zinfandel Sonoma 34.00
1998 Lolonis Zinfandel *Redwood Valley*.......32.00
2000 Karly Zinfandel *Buck's Ten Point*.........32.00
1998 Karly Zinfandel *Warrior Fires*............42.00

Bayfield Breakfast Wars?

Does Freshest & Finest Ingredients Mean Anything?
Does Homemade Everything Mean Anything?
Does Friendly Exotic Atomosphere Mean Anything?
OK OK - So Does 1/2 Off Mean Anything?!
Well then, Get a Coupon Find a Friend & Go for It!

Join the Maggie's Breakfast Club
Eat Breakfast at Maggie's 9 Times
The 10th one is On Us
Includes Coffee or Tea

Or How About This?
Drink Only One Cup of Coffee & Receive a Complimentary Egg Cooked the Way You Like It Whoa Baby!

Breakfast War Bond

Maggie's Breakfast Coupon
Buy One Breakfast get 2nd Breakfast of Equal or lesser Value for 1/2 Price
Includes only Coffee or Tea Folks
Senior Citizens Discount not Applicable
Mon. - Sat.
Redeem at Maggie's Bayfield, WI 779-5641

Look For Your Breakfast War Bonds in the County Journal & The Daily Press

The people make it happen

A HOLE IN MY HEART

Mary introduced me to licorice ice cream, a phenomenal taste! When I first heard that Maggie's was closing I thought that my favorite times and tastes and my wonderful get-togethers with the Queen are gone! I have a hole in my heart, but my memories will never fade. Maggie's was and always will be a special place! Thank you for the memories, Mary!

—Ruth Goetz (pictured above)

BACK BITING

Eons ago, Mike and I located to the Bayfield area. At first we were drawn to the lake and sailing. As time went on, we learned about the wonderful backgrounds of people living nearby or visiting Bayfield. Maggie's was always a weekend stopover with friends: good food, and lots of happy, noisy chatter.

Mike has always been interested in various business ventures and he collaborated with our son Alex in developing engraved products. Soon the "Potty Partners" were in the business of engraving lids of oak toilet seats with representations of the Apostle Islands. In thinking of ways to market the products, Alex came up with the idea of finding high-visibility settings, giving the seats to business owners, and letting the products sell themselves. That's how the adventure began, sitting in Maggie's and pondering the idea.

Sometimes light bulb moments happen on their own. Sometimes it's happenstance, like someone in our table having to use the bathroom: a eureka moment in history.

Sure enough, Mike wound up talking to Mary about a free unique oak toilet seat and she agreed to try it out in the women's restroom. All was going well until the height of tourist season.

Oak toilet seats represent visual luxury, gracing many a home for years. Unfortunately, quality control and substandard glue may be lacking in some brands. Only trial and error can determine the outcome of brand loyalty. High volume settings, like restaurants during the height of a tourist season, can make or break a product. The manager at Maggie's soon gave Mike a desperation call: "the seat is biting our customers!"

The Potty Partners sprang into action and quickly replaced the oak seat with another engraved oak seat, which lasted for years. The guys conducted a forensic analysis of their marketing strategy and decided that their customer base should be family settings where outdoor scenes proved popular.

Looking back over the years, the guys concluded they probably should have field tested their product more carefully, rather than trying to get the attention of customers in Maggie's restaurant.

—Jo and Mike Bailey

BAYFIELD BAR TURNED INTO GOURMET DELIGHT (1981)

It looks like a neighborhood bar on a back street. What if the locals aren't crazy about tourists? "Are you sure this is it?" an innocent-looking mother toting a camera and two daughters said to her husband.

"Well, it doesn't look like much from the outside," muttered the husband, "but it's supposed to have the best food in town."

SITTING ON THE COOLER

I loved Juniors. Would go there with Dad and Junior would let us have a candy or pop. We'd sit on the cooler. He also made the best burgers! *—Jeanne Goodlet-Lemire*

CATER TO LOCALS FIRST

It's been a year since Mary Rice, 41, the owner of a St. Paul gourmet cooking school bought a bar on Bayfield's Manypenny Avenue and started serving food. Out went the old microwave oven that used to turn out palate-scorching pizzas. Rice replaced it with gourmet cookware for poaching fresh fish and simmering soups seasoned with herbs. Maggie's was an instant success.

The locals still hang out at the bar but now they can get 17 imported beers along with a Wisconsin brew on tap. The place seats only 35, but it seems as if everyone wants to be at Maggie's. Rice said she is serving as many as 200 meals a day.

Inside is not much fancier. The tabletops are Formica. But dinner patrons are treated to linen placemats and each table is adorned with a bouquet of fresh flowers.

In addition to owning the restaurant, Mary Rice is co-owner with her sister, Martha Kaemmer, of The Food School at TH'rice, on Grand Avenue in St. Paul. "I hire my teachers for having the most knowledge and the least dogma," said Rice, who has studied at European cooking schools.

She has been a gifted cook for a long time. While other kids were still mixing mud pies, she was baking quiches.

"I've been cooking ever since I was a kid," she said. "My mother let me cook on Saturdays, and it was my family summer job."

She was in charge of the kitchen at their summer home on Sand Island in the Apostles. The rest of the year the family lived in Bayport, Minnesota. There was a lot of entertaining at the summer retreat. Sometimes Rice cooked for 30 or 40 of her family's business associates and friends.

Above: Mary and Phil Sunde (aka Tiny)
Below: kitchen notes

Egg w curry Mayo + Tomato - Rye
Sardine, leaf, Tom sauce, parsley - lem twist
Roast beef w/ Horn + Cuke, Mayo + Sprouts Rye
Steak, Remolaude, Sprouts, white
Steak, horse, H onions - Rye
Pork + beef Pickle + H onions - white
Chicken, horse, beet + Cuke + Sprouts
Salami + Delio + pickle
Cuke, Blue cheese, Nuts
Ham + cheese, Sprouts + Mayo + beet
Beef Tartare, onion Rings Rye
Shrimp, Mayo - Sprouts, Cuke + lemon
Cheese + Herring + Sprouts + beet

Rice's great-grandfather, Hans Jacob, started the Andersen Corp. Her father, William Hulings, is chairman of the company's executive committee.

Maggie's doesn't have to succeed for Rice to pay the bills, yet she works from 10 a.m. to 1 or 2 p.m. daily as if she needed every dime.

"You'd have to be a dumb fool to do this if you didn't love it," she said.

Rice said that after her divorce from a physician, she moved to Bayfield.

"I figured I'd live here when the kids were grown," said Rice, mother of teenagers. "But then I realized I didn't have to wait. I guess this is the first time I thought I had half a chance of doing something I was good at and was rewarding. I didn't want to be Mrs. Volunteer and Mrs. Cooking Teacher the rest of my life. Instead I ended up here working harder than I ever have and I love it."

While she would have considered buying a classier restaurant, Rice bought the place on Manypenny Avenue because it came with a liquor license, which has a reputation for being difficult to acquire in Bayfield. Once she opened, her main goal was to keep the locals feeling comfortable. "It was important to cater to locals first and if we got the outside traffic, that was fine. If you have the local traffic, you've got it made." Her formula seems to be working. "We were busy all winter in a town that doesn't have many people."

—*Peter Maller, September 1981 (excerpts)*

The people make it happen

DALE, IN 1998

Maggie's (famous for flamingo décor) shares services of chef Dale Hanson with The Egg Toss Café, a breakfast restaurant a block away.

"I knew I wanted to be a chef early on. I finished a commercial cooking course and was working at a Radisson kitchen when I was 18 years old," Dale says.

From that beginning, he went on to work at several country clubs, the Minneapolis Athletic Club, and became executive chef at Majestic Oaks Country Club. But he grew dissatisfied with city life.

"We wanted to get out of that rushed lifestyle and looked for opportunities in outlying areas," Dale says. "Two years ago, this position became available. We moved to Bayfield."

The two restaurants are open from 5 a.m. into evening hours. The difference between the summer rush and winter traffic is dramatic. Dale says that Maggie's will do up to 500 covers a day during the summer, while a good winter day may be only about 100.

"Still, we stay open seven days a week year-round and offer dinner specials every day and lunch specials during the summer Our clientele is eclectic and the menu reflects that fact."

This Minnesota native found the lifestyle his family sought when they moved to this friendly Lake Superior community.

CHIPOTLE-LIME CAESAR DRESSING

½ Tsp. cumin
2 shallots, minced
2 ½ Tbsp Dijon mustard
2 Tbsp fresh cilantro, minced
6 chipotle chilis, hydrated, seeded, minced
6 egg yolks
8 anchovy fillets
¼ Cup shredded parmesan
2 Tbsp balsamic vinegar
1 1/3 cup olive oil
½ Cup lime juice
2/3 Cup corn oil
½ Tsp kosher salt
¼ Tsp cayenne pepper

In a food processor, puree all but the oils, salt and cayenne pepper until incorporated. Add oils slowly to form a mayonnaise. Season with salt and cayenne.

—excerpted from a 1998 article

WHEN DALE MET MARY

I waited at a farm house in the country to meet with Mary Rice, to talk about possibly becoming the chef at her flagship restaurant, Maggie's. I had never met Mary before and did not know what to expect. My first impression, as I sat in my car with Molly's Great Dane barking at me through the driver's window with its paws resting on the car, was that, "this should be interesting." Not taking any chances, I waited in my car until someone (hopefully) would come out. No one did. As I was waiting, Mary pulled into the driveway, introduced herself, and assured me that the dog did not bite. Over the next hour in Molly's living room, we talked about food, travel, the restaurant world, and dreams about the future. Within the next few months I would pick up stakes and move to little old Bayfield and spend the next 13 years working for Mary, traveling with Mary, and most importantly, eating with and learning from Mary. Her knowledge about food and pretty much anything else was voluminous. Mary turned out to be my boss, mentor, and most importantly a friend. I owe her for my own business, my beautiful wife Lois, and the pleasures of living in a truly great place. I will never forget her humor, generosity, and playfulness that all who knew her can attest to. R.I P. Mary Rice, gone but never forgotten.

—Dale Hanson.

Dale Hanson and Lois Stensvad: longtime employees of Maggie's

Above: Kenny Dobson with Mary's architect Wayne Spangler. Below left: Bill VanSant, Craig Johnson, Marilyn VanSant, Sharon Johnson. Below right: Teresa Polaski. Tom Polaski and Joyce Bratti

Top: Jimmy Smith and Mary. Above: Cecilia Duquette, Barb Spencer. Below: Tom Polaski and Ed Olson

THE TRUTH COMES OUT!

In the early eighties, I worked at Maggie's Saturday mornings for the breakfast crowd with Debbie Erickson Bresette who was the chef. The other job I had was a night shift from 11 p.m. to 7 a.m. So, when I got to Maggie's, I had already worked a full day and was, of course, very tired but working with Debbie always made it fun.

One particular Saturday morning, I arrived at 7:20 for my breakfast shift but the restaurant looked like Friday night had been wild. Debbie and I worked quickly to get things ready. She plugged the jukebox in and it started to play, "Wasn't That a Party" by the Irish Rovers. That set me off in a crazy tired direction and it didn't take much to get Debbie on board with me. I honestly do not remember how or who did it, but a bottle of Jim Beam landed in front of us, two shot glasses followed, and we started our morning with Jimmie Beam! By 8 a.m., we were quite happy! Debbie was in the kitchen with Jimmie Beam and I waited on people.

When I brought orders back to the kitchen, Debbie strangely asked who they were for so I started writing names on the orders. One customer, known to be very loud, ordered buckwheat pancakes. **After several bites, he started exclaiming that these were the best pancakes he had ever eaten**; everyone should order them! Other customers (who

Above: Heidi Nelson, Rich Ryan and Jim Webster

we definitely knew) ordered them and agreed that the pancakes were excellent. It became the talk of the restaurant. I went back to the kitchen and **asked Debbie what the heck was making the pancakes so good this morning.** She smiled, picked up the bottle and said, "I put a little Jimmie in the batter." We laughed so hard, we almost pissed in our pants. Then we had another drink (or two) of Jimmie Beam, our morning date.

—*Kristin Edwards Connell (below with Gary)*

Above: Jim Webster, Melissa Newago

FELT LIKE FAMILY COMING TOGETHER

When Mary Rice first bought Juniors bar, the biggest changes were flamingos, a new coat of paint (mostly pink), the train that circled the ceiling, and a new sense of FUN. In the early years, **there might have been some food served but it was really mostly a fun drinking bar.** By day, you could usually find Mary at her favorite booth, conducting business, holding court, and conversing with all who dropped by.

"A guy nobody knew" known as Dick Head for his talent of putting a condom on his head and blowing it up; the crowd went crazy!

A favorite memory about those years are what happened when a big snowstorm hit and everything was closed. We all headed to Maggie's to do some day drinking and partying and celebrating the day off! People came on foot, on skis, by snowmobile, by car—ones that could make it through the snow and some that couldn't—in which case a few guys would be dispatched to rescue or at least get them to the bar. It gave us a feeling of camaraderie and reason to celebrate overcoming such adversity. We were safe and warm with friends and neighbors, and only grins ahead.

Eventually, we would all (or up to 20 of us) end up dancing on the pool table singing something like "My Sharona" at the top of our lungs. Mary had a wooden "dance floor" made by Kenny Dobson to fit the table because there was just no room to dance anywhere else. People who serviced the pool table were always mad at Mary because the center support would rub off the felt; it had to be replaced several times. I loved that Mary didn't care or listen to them! She loved it when we'd pull her up to join in!

Maggie's also hosted "beauty pageants" which drew locals dressed in pageant costumes, all tongue-in-cheek of course. Debbie Weber entered into those at least twice that I remember. In the first one, she wore a satin nightgown of Mary's and created a character around it using a deep purple body suit underneath, a bathing cap, and a large stuffed ass, along with a unique "walk" (a la Big Butt Sisters from SNL). That was the night that a guy, unknown to us, sat on the pool table, put a condom over his head and proceeded to blow it up for the talent competition! Kenny Dobson was always in when it came to costuming too; he would pick something so no one could recognize him. One Halloween, he was dressed in a full ape suit (or a bear, I can't remember) and he would just lurk around and grunt out a few comments as we all tried to figure out who it was. He stayed in character the whole night and, after he left, it was only through the process of elimination that we guessed his identity.

I think it was around the time when Mary bought Bates Bar that the parties, music, and events (Come As Your Favorite Tourist parties every September) moved to that larger venue, and Mary ramped up the food at Maggie's. So our beloved pool table was removed and the expansion for more seating was done. It became more known and visited for the good food and over-the-top décor. It was a great restaurant in Bayfield for many years! But I will say that I missed our party place, probably because it was so intimate and small, it felt like family coming together.

—Jan Esposito

Below: Roger Bristol

The people make it happen

THE NEXT BOOTH

My friend was helping me hang pictures
but we didn't have the hooks we needed.
It was Sunday afternoon
and the hardware store was closed.
The junk store did not have any.

The grocery store did not have any.
So, screw it, we went to Maggie's to eat lunch
where, in the off season, everyone is acquainted.

My friend said hello to Willy in the next booth.
I didn't know him.

Then we had a conversation
about the hooks, with the waitress,
in which the term
well hung got tossed about.

The conversation shifted, we got our meal.

Suddenly Willy was at our table.
He said he couldn't help overhearing us,
so he had gone home,
found what we needed in his garage
and handed picture hangers to us
all neat in a little baggie.

—*Ros Nelson*

OWNER'S DREAM

"It's a corner pub with good food." That's how owner Mary Rice describes her newly-purchased tavern, "Maggie's" at 3rd and Manypenny in Bayfield. She bought the establishment, formerly known as Fisherman's Cove, in August and since that time has done some remodeling.

Ros Nelson and Mary

Flamingo Tenders

Sauce

1 cup	Frank's RedHot Original Cayenne Pepper Sauce
¼ #	Butter
¼ Tbsp	Cajun Seasoning
Pinch	Cayenne Pepper

Combine all ingredients in a saucepan and heat thoroughly over medium heat.

Chicken Strips

Slice lengthwise 3-4 boneless chicken breasts. Dredge in a mixture of ½ cup flour, 1 tsp salt and 1 tsp pepper.
Heat ½ cup frying oil to hot in a skillet and quick fry strips until done. (If you have a deep fryer do them in that.)
Pour sauce over to cover and serve.

"I've been coming to Bayfield since I was four years old and I love it, I have always wanted to run a place of my own." Before purchasing the Bayfield pub, she ran the Pots and Pans store and a cooking school in St. Paul. She taught the art of making "all kinds of cuisine," she adds.

Visitors to Maggie's can order a homemade pizza—not pre-packaged—made on the premises. The 9" house special includes tomato sauce, green pepper, onion, green olives, mozzarella cheese and a choice of pepperoni, salami, or ground beef, or all three. The cost of the pizza depends on how many extras are added, she explains. The regular menu includes, burgers, fresh cut French fries, onion rings and homemade potato chips. Sandwiches include Italian sausage, grilled cheese, grilled ham and cheese, pizza in a crust and Maggie's twin—a choice of roast beef, corned beef, turkey or ham on white, onion, rye, or pumpernickel. Patrons can order salads, soups, luscious ice cream and drinks like hot apple cider, hot buttered rum, or a Tom and Jerry.

Every Monday night is Ethnic Night at Maggie's. German and Scandinavian dinners are planned in the future.

A Christmas party has been scheduled at the Bayfield tavern starting at 3 p.m. on Sunday, Dec. 21. Although Ms. Rice has worked long hours getting her business into shape, she says that running the pub is what she expected and she's glad she made the move. The bar is open from 10 a.m. to 1 a.m., Monday through Saturday and from 1 p.m. to 1 a.m., Sunday.

—*Bayfield County Press*

FLAMINGOS CROSS STATE LINES

When Buzz and I drove from our cabin at Chub Lake, near Cloquet, to visit Mary in the early '80s, we delighted in learning about Maggie's. Of course we ate there, enjoying great food and hospitality, and we could see the beginnings of a unique decorative venture that would, in itself, draw people from across the country. Its style was bold and quirky, and there was a zany emphasis on flamingos.

I realized we could contribute to that décor. We'd inherited two black-and-flamingo'd tin trays, the tops of TV tables (pg. 139), and I'd always thought them really ghastly, so we brought them to Bayfield on our next visit. They were well received and, you know, they looked just right at Maggie's! We've enjoyed seeing them on every visit since. Our last visit there was two years ago, a supper with Mary, John Hanson, and my sister. Mary was in good form. We had lively conversations over our whitefish, and relished brief chats with others who stopped by to greet Mary. It's a good memory to think of her there, in her element, my extraordinary friend. We salute Maggie's 40th, and send hearty wishes to all.

—Janet Foster Carroll

appetizer Line Pre[p]

	total	on hand
Black Bean puree	2 1/4 Pans	
green chile Sauce	2 1/4 Pans	
Livers	1 1/4 Pan	
mushrooms	1 1/4 Pan ~~1 1/4 Pan~~ & Bag	
onions & Peppers	1	
cheddar & M. Jack	2	
tarter Sauce	1 1/2 Pan	
Blue cheese dressing	1 sheet Pan	
tarragon Sauce	1 1/2 Pan	
Flamingo sauce	2 1/4 Pans	
Roast garlic	1 Bucket	
Polenta cut	2 containers	
Polenta sheet pans	2 1/2 sheet Pans	
chicken tenders	4 Qts	
Leaf Lettuce	4 Qts	
Fresh Salsa	4 Qts	
Naches	3 Buckets	
tortilla chip cut Blue	4 Qts	
Red	4 Qts	
yellow	4 Qts	

COUPLE FAVORITE MEMORIES

– Playing 7, 14, 21 and hoping you didn't land on 21, especially when someone picked something gross like cherry brandy or Slivovitz (plum brandy)!

– Staying with Mary until closing and then going to her house for garbage omelets. (Unfortunately, Mary took the food for our omelets from Maggie's, so when the morning cook came in there was nothing prepped!)

– And who can forget the wonderful Magical Mystery Bus Tours! From Packer games to jazz clubs, we certainly had our share of fun. Thank you, Mary for the many adventures, and thanks for the memories!

—Sharon Wszalek

Maggie's 25th anniversary celebration!

Saturday, august 20th in maggie's parking lot

TASTY SPECIALS! think pink!

THINK PINK!

Fun & flamingos fun & flamingos fun & flamingos fun & flamingos

Come join us starting with our maggie's Parade at 11:00 a.m. followed by music, Fun, food, and thirst quenchers in our Very own parking lot!! (music from 1:00 til 4:00 p.m. (free munchies in the parking lot)● ●

Music by marky baby (however there is no **And sasha Mercedes!!!!!!!!!!!!!** free lunch!)● ● ●-------

MORE FUN AND MORE FLAMINGOS!

Join in on all the fun and think pink at the pink palace.
Our very own queen mary will be here!!!!!!!!!!!!!!!!!!!!!!!!!!!!
And so should you!!

Heidi Nelson and Mary

Mary Kay Defoe and Mary Rice

Below: Lloyd Turner, Denise Koch, Diane Brander

Another day, another parade!

25th anniversary

Above: Margie Erickson. Lower left: Mary Kay Defoe with 25th year sign. Lower right: Mary's sandals!

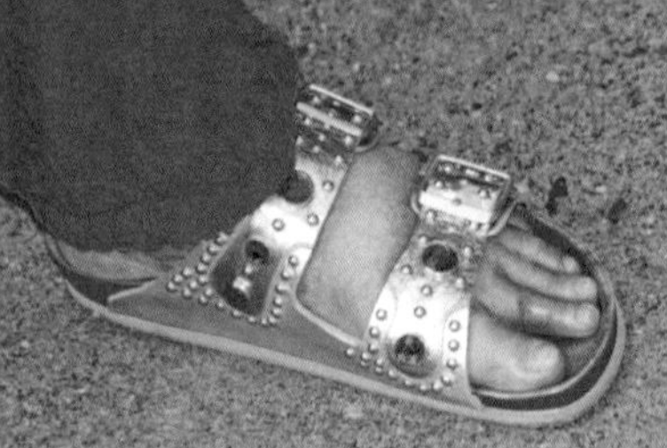

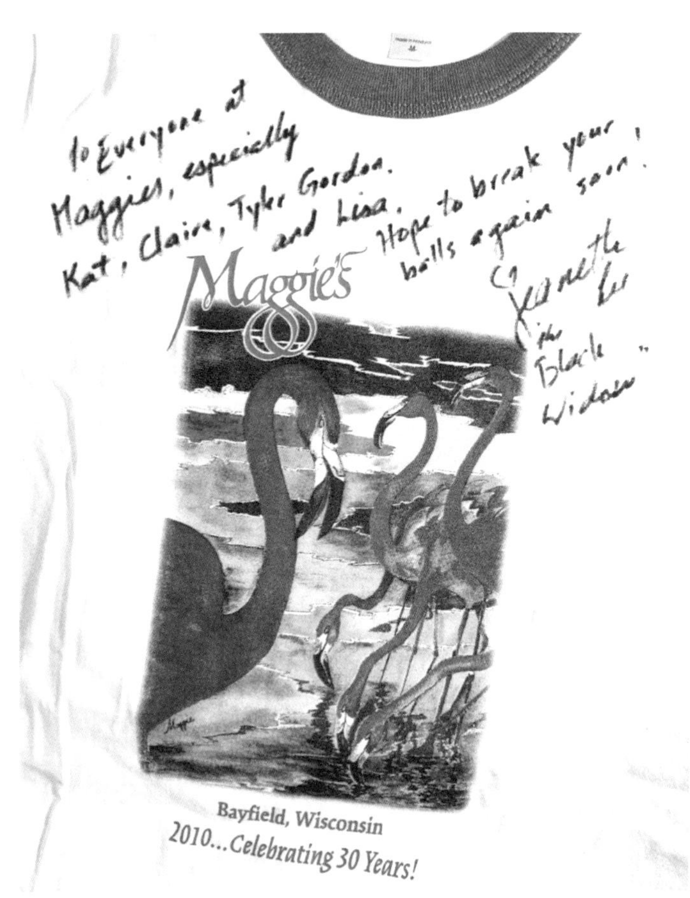

Far left top and bottom: Brenda Erickson

Lower middle: Kylie and Sue Glover

Maggie's

Pink Palace

Celebrating FlamingoLand 2010

Still Flapping After 30 Years... We're Tough Old Birds!

Your support speaks volumes...

and laughs and giggles, and shouts too. **One percent is all it takes.** This establishment proudly participates in the voluntary **1% for Recreation Program** created to raise funds for the Bayfield Recreation Center. Your 1% donation will automatically appear on your dinner check. Please tell your waitron if you would like this 1% donation removed from your check. Thanks for your support.

Welcome To

Thank you for joining our celebration! Maggie's is 30 Years Old! For the next thirty years, we hope to continue to provide you with the great food and excellent service to which you've not only become accustomed, but that you deserve.

In celebration of this milestone, you'll notice a little bit of a change in our menu. We're continuing to offer your favorite Maggie's Traditional selections of course, but as you'll see, we've added a "FlamingoLand @ Night Section. You'll find it on the back page.

The "@ Night" Section features all new creative experiments that we hope will get added to your list of favorites as we flamingos fly forth. All of our innovations were summoned from the curious culinary mind of Tiny, our Executive Chef.

Home-Grown & Home-Made...

With any entrée, just ask us for a plate of this morning's **Egg Toss**-baked fresh bread assortment

All of our salad dressings are **made right here in-house** (Home-Made salad dressings include French, Ranch, Italian, Bleu Cheese, Raspberry Vinaigrette, and Vinegar & Oil. All of the berries and most of the produce Maggie's uses are **locally grown**. We only use the **freshest available ingredients** in all of our entrees, and where and whenever possible, we buy as much as we can locally. It's good for you, good for our community, and good for our world.

How-a Bout-a Bowl-o-Cozy...

All of Maggie's soups are **lovingly brewed from scratch,** in our own cauldrons, using the **freshest ingredients** available.

Please check our dining room chalkboards for the daily offerings.

Maggie's Most Excellent Chili	3.00 For A Cup, 3.50 For A Bowl
Broth Soups	3.00 For A Cup, 3.50 For A Bowl
Cream Soups	3.00 For A Cup, 3.50 For A Bowl

OUR SPECIAL MEXICAN TORTILLA SOUP – 5.50
Smoky homemade broth seasoned with lime juice, house-smoked chicken, cilantro, fried tortilla strips

...And In The End, Sweetness!

Maggie's pies, cakes, tarts, and tortes are crafted every morning by our own **Egg Toss Bakery**.
Our crème brulee is sooo smooth—simply amazing!
Karmyn's ice creams are incredible, and are made right here at Maggie's.
All fruit pies and other fruit-topped desserts feature local Bayfield berries when in season.

Chocolate Flourless Torte -------------------- 6.00
New York Cheesecake -------------------------- 5.50
Maggie's Own Crème Brulee ------------------ 5.50
Home-Baked Fruit Pie -------------------------- 4.50
Karmyn's Ice Cream Sampler ------------------ 5.50

Don't Forget Our Lucky 7 Lunches... And...

On A Cold, Winters' Night...

Tuesdays --- Family Style Night
Portioned & priced for your family size
19.95 for 2, 26.95 for 3, 32.95 for 4.
Add 6.95 per person for parties of 5 or more.

Wednesdays --- Half-Priced Burgers
Choose any of our 8oz. Burgers for half the price. Includes chips and a pickle.

Thursdays --- Thirsty Thursday!
Half-priced bottle of wine of your choice with any entrée purchased.

Fridays --- All You Can Eat Fish Fry
Featuring beer-battered Lake Superior Bluefin Herring. Served with fries and coleslaw.

Please pay your server.
A 20% service charge may be added to parties of eight or more.

To ensure prompt service for all, we ask that you not request separate checks for parties of six or more.

Maggie's Gift Cards make great gifts—
that's why they're called gift cards.
Don't forget Maggie's Mugs & T-shirts, too!

Always a critical stop on our annual "Nap and Cocktail" tour of Lake Superior. —*Amanda and Lindsay Wood Davis, Monona, Wisconsin*

Celebrating FlamingoLand 2010

Still Flapping After 30 Years...
We're Tough Old Birds!

Celebrating Fond Memories
Of 30 Years Gone By...
Just A Walk In The Park!

Bayfield, Wisconsin
2010...Celebrating 30 Years!

HUGE SHRIMP EVERYWHERE

My dad, Al Franzen, took me to one of her Christmas school parties at her house. She had huge shrimp everywhere and I thought I could eat them all! She was very generous and my dad and I had a wonderful time
—Kimberly Franzen-Reynolds

Angus Management...

Maggie's uses **USDA Choice** 5 oz. and 8 oz. **Angus** burger patties. Burgers cooked rare, medium rare, or pink in the middle may be undercooked and are served only upon request.
CONSUMER ADVISORY: The consumption of raw or undercooked potentially hazardous foods can cause illness.

FEELING GLUTTONOUS? DOUBLE THE 8 OZ. PATTY FOR ONLY 5.00 MORE! IT'S SINFUL!

The "Infamous" Plain Ol' Burger – 5 oz., 6.25 – 8 oz., 7.50
No frills, just greatness

Maggie's Good-Ol' Cheeseburger – 5 oz., 7.00 – 8 oz., 8.25
Aged cheddar, colby, Amish blue, Swiss OR mozzarella

All-American Burger – 5 oz., 7.50 – 8 oz., 8.75
With apple smoked bacon and aged cheddar

Mushroom Swiss Burger – 5 oz., 7.25 – 8 oz., 8.50
Just what it says, folks

Black & Blue Burger – 5 oz., 7.25 – 8 oz. 8.50
Blackened burger with blue cheese

President Burger – 5 oz., 7.50 – 8 oz., 8.75
President Brie cheese and caramelized onion

Lotsa Cheese Burger – 5 oz., 7.75 – 8 oz., 9.00
"You know you're in Wisconsin now!" With cheddar, Swiss, Colby and bacon
(Call your Dr. before Ordering)

The "WILD WEST" Bison Burger – 5 oz., 7.25
Bison patty topped with pepper-jack cheese.
Served with sandwich pickle slice and Maggie's own cumin barbeque sauce

Maggie's own Veritable, Voluptuous, Veggie Burger – 8 oz., 9.00
Bulgar, buck and barley berries, parmesan cheese, broccoli,
sun-dried tomatoes, onion and garlic ALL home-made GOOD!

Make your burger California Style with Lettuce, Tomato and Onion, **add 1.25**

All burgers and some sandwiches include chips and a pickle. Need extra sauce? **Only .50**
Wanna trade your chips for Home-Cut Fries? **Add 1.75** Sweet Potato Fries instead of chips? **Add 2.50**

A Pig, A Cow & A

Walk Into A Bar... (Can you guess the punch line?)

In-House-Smoked Beef Brisket Sandwich – 11.00
Served hot and piled high, with red onion and our own crunchy, tangy cole slaw

Flamingo Chicken Sandwich – 9.00
Fried boneless breast, dipped in our flamingo hot sauce and served on a grilled bun
with shredded lettuce, onion and blue cheese dressing

Pork Chimichanga – 9.50
Mexican style shredded pork and cheddarjack cheese? in a fried flour tortilla,
served with lettuce, cheese, fresh salsa, sour cream, black beans and rice

Chicken Fajitas – 12.00
"A Maggie's tradition!" Garlic-lime marinated chicken breast, grilled with onions and peppers
with tortillas, sour cream, cheddar cheese, fresh salsa, black beans and rice

n The Beginning...

Maggie's Legendary
Re-Fried Black Bean Nachos – 8.25
"These are great!" Corn tortillas,
cheddar and Monterey jack cheeses,
black olives, green onions, sour cream & pico de gallo

Flamingo Tenders – 8.00
Seasoned flour-dusted chicken breast strips
Sautéed in our own hot pepper sauce
and served with a blue cheese dressing

Whitefish Livers – 8.50
A local specialty! Dredged in seasoned cornmeal, and
sauteed with mushrooms, onions and peppers

Locally Brown Sugar Smoked Trout Salsa – 9.00
Perched on a bed of spring greens and served with tortilla chips

Flamingo Food Cocktail – 9.50
If it's good for them, it's good for us! (It's Shrimp)
Served with roasted vegetable sauce

Sidelines

Black Beans & Rice – 6.50
Sour cream, cheddar cheese, onions and salsa

Garlic Polenta Fries – 6.00
"Crispy goodness"

Home-Cut French Fries – 3.50

Hand Cut Sweet Potato Fries – 5.50
Sprinkled with sea salt and
served with tarragon sauce

Crunchy, Tangy Cole Slaw – 3.50
Mmm...

Carefully Cultivated...

Mixed Baby Greens – 5.00
Choice of Maggie's Italian, French, blue cheese, ranch, vinegar & oil,
or raspberry flamingo dressing, all lovingly made in our kitchen

Mary & Marilyn's Salad – 4.50
Fresh, crunchy carrots, broccoli and cauliflower tossed with our own Italian dressing

Mediterranean Salad – 9.50 - With Grilled Chicken – 12.00
Organic greens garnished with vine ripe tomato, kalamata olives,
feta cheese, cucumbers, red onion and fresh basil

Caesar Salad – 9.50 - With Grilled Chicken – 12.00
"The Classic"

Locally Brown Sugar Smoked Whitefish Salad – 12.00
Served on a bed of fresh, baby spinach, hard-boiled egg, red onion and cucumber

Black and Blue Chicken Salad – 12.00
Cajun seasoned char-grilled chicken breast and Danish blue cheese on
a mixed green salad with tomato, cucumber and red onion

Strawberry Fields... or maybe Raspberry or... Blueberry or... 9.00 - With Grilled Chicken – 11.50
Mixed baby greens, red onion, fresh Strawberries (when in season from Bayfield's own fruit farms)
and toasted almonds with lemon-poppy seed dressing

2 Things To Noodle

Italian Ties – 15.00
Bow-Tie pasta with a blanket of sauteed shrimp, peppers, onions and capers in an olive oil and white wine sauce

Spicy Red Curry Pasta – 12.50 - With Grilled Chicken – 15.00
Bow-Tie pasta topped with red curried broccoli, cauliflower, carrots, peppers and onions

A Little On The Flaky Side...

They swam in Apostle waters last night... Fresh every morning, from fish monger Morris, in his 89th year

Maggie's Superior Sandwich – 9.00
Morris' fresh Lake Trout or Whitefish, broiled or sauteed. Served on a bun with our own tangy tarter

Simply Fish Dinner – 16.00
Lake Trout or Whitefish, sautéed, broiled, or cedar planked. Served with our own tangy tartar,
Egg Toss fresh baked bread, an organic baby greens salad, and
your choice of black beans and rice, roasted baby red potatoes or French fries

Lake Superior Whitefish Liver Dinner – 15.00
Dredged through seasoned cornmeal, sauteed with mushrooms, onions and peppers.
Served with roasted baby red potatoes or black beans and rice

Livin' The Pie Life...

Maggie's pizzas feature home-made, Wisconsin style dough, rolled to order.
Every pizza is topped with the finest ingredients available.

Just Cheese – 10", 7.00 – 12", 9.00

Add Extra Ingredients – 10" – Add 2.00 each, 12" – Add 2.50 each

Cheeses: mozzarella, cheddar, Parmesan, asiago, feta

Veggies: Onions, spinach, bell pepper, jalapeno, black olives, green olives
Fresh mushrooms, roast peppers, anchovies, artichokes

Meats: Italian sausage, pepperoni, chicken, bacon, Canadian bacon

Vegetable Pizza – 10", 11.00 – 12", 14.75
"A Veggie-Head gotta-have!" Spinach, mushrooms, onions, green bell peppers,
artichoke hearts, tomatoes, mozzarella, asiago and Parmesan cheeses

Greek Salad Pizza – 10", 11.00 – 12", 14.75
Olive oil, tomato, Greek olives, feta and Parmesan cheeses, topped with a salad of
baby organic greens, cucumbers, red onion, lemon scented Italian dressing

BBQ Chicken Pizza – 10", 11.00 – 12", 14.75
Maggie's own Cumin BBQ sauce, in-house smoked chicken, red onion and Monterey Jack cheese

The Late Night Special – 10", 11.00 – 12", 15.00
Pesto, chicken, tomato, fresh Parmesan and feta cheeses

In-House Smoked Chicken and Brie Cheese – 10", 11.00 – 12", 15.00
Caramelized onions, roasted red peppers and Parmesan cheese

Maggie's House Special – 10", 11.00 – 12", 15.00
Tomato sauce, green olives, green peppers, onions, tomatoes, pepperoni and sausage

A Pig, A Cow & A

Walk Into A Bar... (Can you guess the punch line?)

In-House-Smoked Beef Brisket Sandwich – 10.00
Served hot and piled high, with red onion and our own crunchy, tangy cole slaw

Flamingo Chicken Sandwich – 9.00
Fried boneless breast, dipped in our flamingo hot sauce and served on a grilled bun
with shredded lettuce, onion and blue cheese dressing

Pork Chimichanga – 9.50
Mexican style shredded pork and cheddarjack cheese? in a fried flour tortilla,
served with lettuce, cheese, fresh salsa, sour cream, black beans and rice

Chicken Fajitas – 12.00
"A Maggie's tradition!" Garlic-lime marinated chicken breast, grilled with onions and peppers
with tortillas, sour cream, cheddar cheese, fresh salsa, black beans and rice

Long Live The Queen...

Happy 30th Maggie's!

Happy 70th Mary!

None are so old as those
who have outlived enthusiasm.
-- **Henry David Thoreau**

This year, 2010, Maggie's celebrates its 30th year. Our own Queen Mary celebrates her 70th year. Some might think, "Wow, that'sa lottsa years. Now that would depend on your perspective, wouldn't it? We're here to tell ya folks… We're Just Gettin' Started! Look Out! We're as Enthusiastic about Sharing our Fun and Excitement as we've Ever Been. And we have YOU to thank for it! That's right… You, our guests, are what drives our enthusiasm, and we do thank you. We hope you'll be with us as we venture forth to see what surprises lurk in the future of FlamingoLand. (See, Henry, We ain't so old.)

Early menus

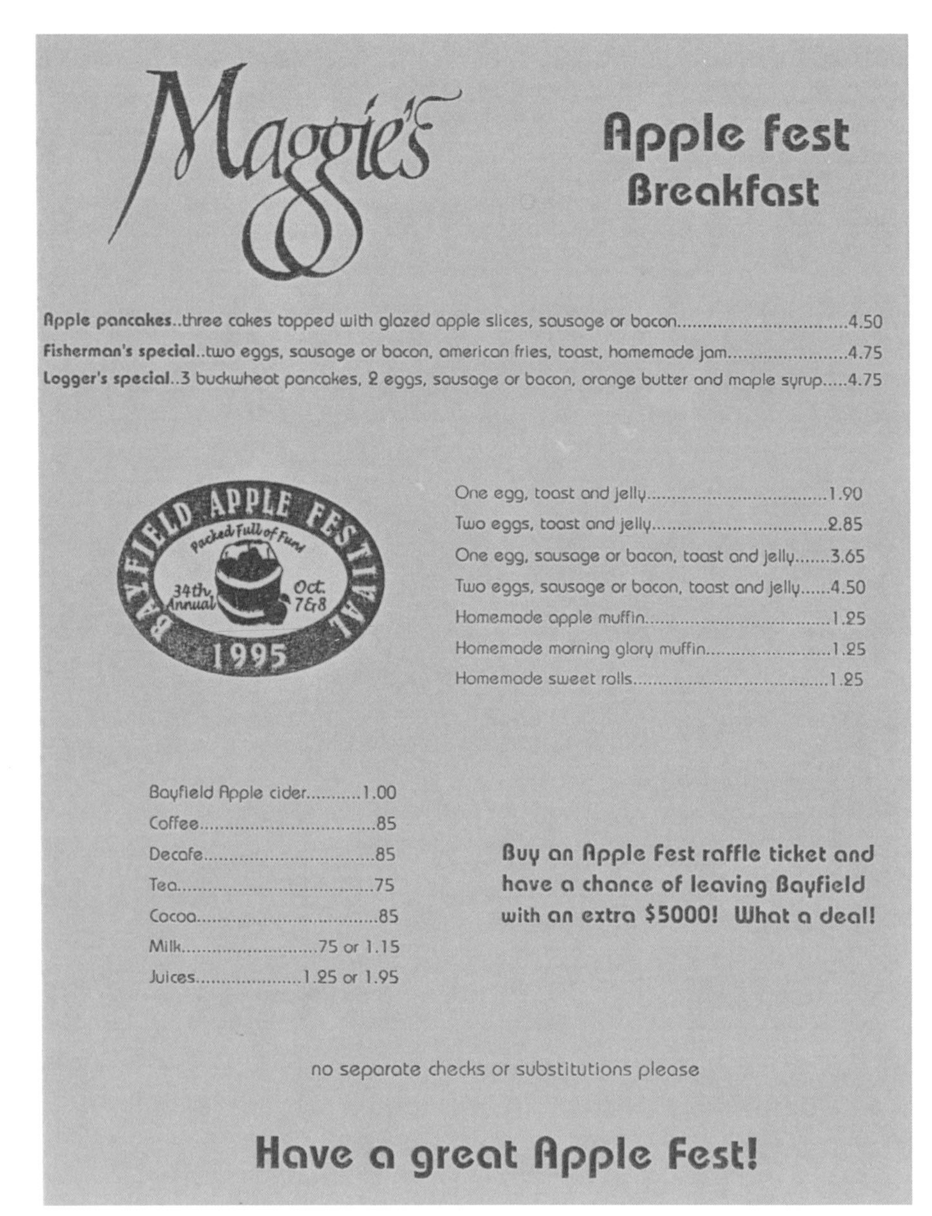

PAID!

Our family went to eat at Maggie's. I had a job interview and told a waitress who had been there over 20 years. I think her name was Mary. My boss Don Mon was there also and he came over and I introduced him. We talked and finished up and when I asked our waitress for the check, she said someone paid for it! Enjoy! I knew who it was. —*Christie Branagan*

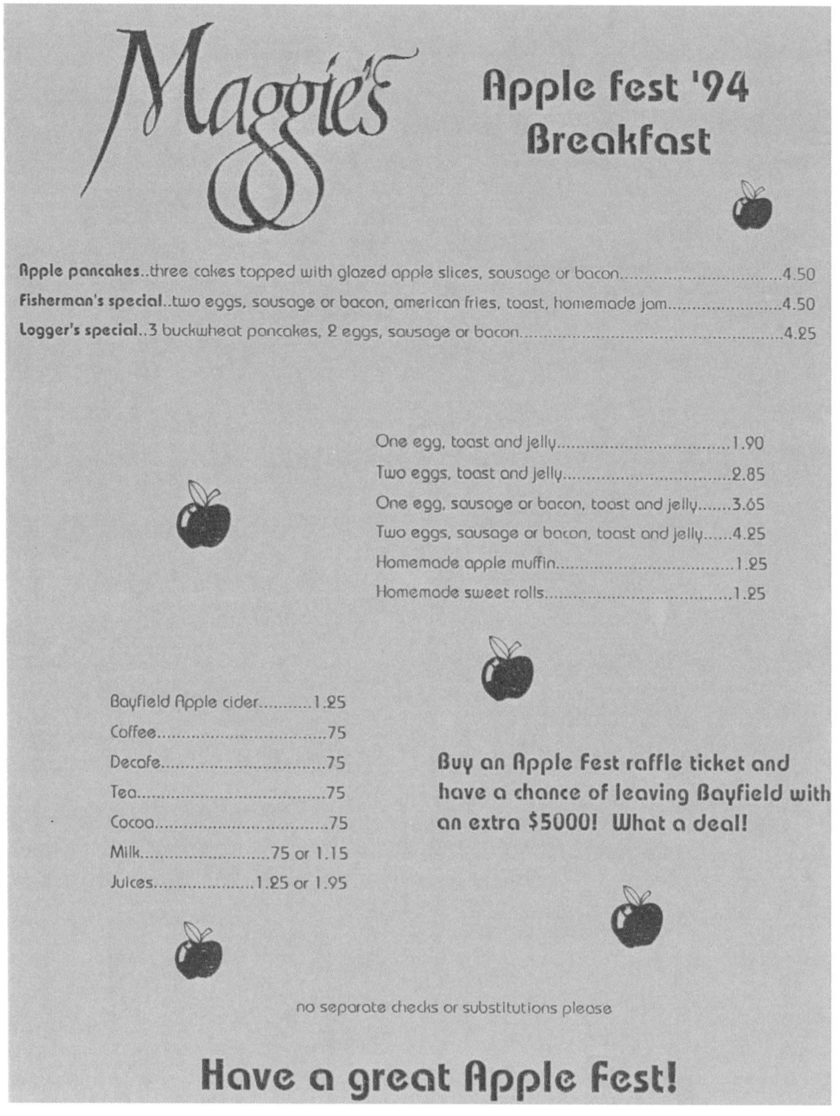

The people make it happen

Tues. Eve

Fried Chick	Baked Potatoes
Steak Sand	Green beans
Fish Poach	Chips
Fry	Fries
NY Strips	Cuke Salad
Jose Mondragon Tostada	Rasp Shtcake Sundae
	Whiz banger

Wednesday

Chicken Caccia	Baked
Steak Sand	Chips
Fish Poach	Fries
Fry	Sauteed Zucchini
Tenderloins	Cuke Salad
Moussaka (no meat)	Rasp Shtcake Sundae
	Whiz banger

JOIN US!

Maggie's was our go-to, favorite restaurant from its inception. When we stepped inside and Mary was hosting a dinner party, we would happily be summoned for inclusion. At that point, we knew we were in for a raucous, calorie-filled evening.

Celebrities were often guests of honor and we were delighted to share the dinner table. At one point, Mary had invited Robin Williams' brother, Robert Williams to town to advertise his winery, Toad Hollow Vineyards. Wine tasting, elegant cuisine, stories, and humor were the order of that evening. More recently, we found ourselves joining the family of Julia Child's sister. Mary's many connections contributed to her incredible, larger-than-life story and her generosity afforded many opportunities for friends. So many more stories to be told … but that's for another book.

—Love, Barbara and John McFarland

Top: Mark Rossow, aka Markie Baby. Above: Stephanie Bresette, Heidi Nelson, Phil Sunde (aka Tiny)

At left, l-r: Vicki and Paul Lambrecht, John and Barbara McFarland

Below: Mary, Ros Nelson, unknown, Stephanie Bresette

Maggie's

LUNCH

APPETIZERS

FRENCH FRIES 5-6oz .90
GERMAN FRIES 5oz .90
HOMEMADE CHIPS .90
CLASSIC CHIPS .90

ONION RINGS
WHITEFISH LIV
CHICKEN WINGS
sweet & sour

MAGGIE'S INTERNATIONAL BURGERS

USA EAST 3.15
hamburger, french fries, pickle
with cheese .25 extra

USA WEST
california burger, french f
with cheese .25 extra

CANADIAN BURGER 3.75
canadian bacon, swiss cheese on a beef
pattie, french fries

GERMAN BURGER
homemade sauerkraut on a be
pickle, german fries

MEXICAN BURGER 3.50
cheese and refried beans on a beef
pattie, topped with hot sauce and
sour cream, taco chips

GREEK BURGER
marinated black olives, oni
tomatoes, feta cheese on a
served on pita bread

CIA BURGER 3.75
swiss, colby, blue cheese or cheddar
cheese, mozarella and pepperoni inside
a beef pattie, french fries

IRISH BURGER
corned beef, cheddar cheese
pattie, horseradish sauce, c
chips

ITALIAN BURGER 3.50
pizza sauce, pepperoni, mozarella cheese
on a beef pattie, homemade chips

DANISH BURGER
shredded pot roast in beer
sauce, classic chips, pickle

FRENCH BURGER 3.50
mushrooms, red onion and blue cheese
on a beef pattie, french fries

ENGLISH BURGER
fresh Lake Superior whitefi
deepfried, on a bun, homema

BURGERS

HAMBURGER 2.25
CHEESEBURGER 2.50
CALIFORNIA BURGER 2.75
CALIFORNIA CHEESEBURGER 3.00
all burgers served with potato chips,
pickle

SALADS

TOSSED GARDEN SALAD
MAGGIE'S CHEF SALAD
ITALIAN VEGETABLE SALAD
GREEK SALAD
italian or french dressing
1000 island .50 blue chees

'WICHES

GRILLED CHEESE 1.75
GRILLED HAM AND CHEESE 2.50
HAM OR TURKEY 2.25
ROAST SIRLOIN TIP 2.50
served with your choice of white, whole
wheat or rye bread, potato chips, pickle

BISCUITS

BISCUIT AND BUTTER
BISCUIT, BUTTER AND CHEESE
ADD ON:
TOMATO, ONION OR LETTUCE
EGG OR TURKEY
SAUSAGE OR BACON

NO SUBSTITUITIONS PLEASE!

Maggies Beverages

United States 1.10

Budweiser
Budweiser light
Coors
Coors light
Leinenkugel
Miller
Miller lite
Old Milwaukee
Old Style
Old Style L.A.
Pabst
Stroh's

Premiums 1.20

Andeker
Augsberger
Augsberger Dk
Michelob
Michelob light
Special Export

On Tap

Augsberger .55 - .75
Hacker Pschorr .90 1.50 2.00
pitcher Augsberger 4.00
pitcher Hacker Pschorr 8.00

Non Alcoholic

Kingsbury 1.10
Moussy 2.00

Pop and Mineral Water

Coke diet Coke Sprite .35 .40 .75
tonic club soda .35 .40 .75
ginger ale .75
LaCroix 1.00

Coffee, Tea and Juices

Cameron's Gourmet Blend Coffee .60
Cameron's Columbian Decafe .75
juices 1.25 1.95
lemonade .75
iced tea .50

Canada

LaBatt's Blue 1.65
Molson Golden 1.65
Moosehead 1.65

China

Tsing Tao 2.50

Czechoslavakia

Pilsner Urquell 2.00

Denmark

Carlsberg Elephant 2.25

England

Bass Ale 2.50
Whitbread Ale 2.50

Germany

Beck's light 2.25
Beck's Dark 2.25
Dunkel Acker 2.50
Hacker Pschorr Weiss 3.00
St Pauli light 2.25
St Pauli Dark 2.25

Holland

Amstel light 2.50
Grolsch 16oz 3.00
Heineken 2.25

Ireland

Guiness Stout 2.50
Harp Lager 2.50

Mexico

Corona Extra 2.25
Dos Equis 2.00
Negra Modelo 2.50

Norway

Ringnes 2.50

Wine

Bartles and Jaymes 2.00
Riunite Lambrusco 1.50
Paul Masson Burgundy
Sebastiani Chablis, Rose, Rhin
Carafe 7.95 glass 1.50

Early menus

BREAKFAST

Maggie's

A.M. RUSH-ham, 2 eggs, swiss cheese served on a homemade biscuit 3.25

ECSTASY SANDWICH-2 slices of french toast filled with cream cheese, syrup and butter 3.00

FISHERMAN'S SPECIAL-2 eggs, sausage/bacon, hash browns, toast and jelly 3.50

LOGGERS SPECIAL-3 buckwheats, 2 eggs, sausage/bacon 3.25

HUEVOS RANCHEROS-flour tortilla, refried beans, 2 eggs, colby cheese, sauce, sour cream 3

on Saturday's only-COTTAGE CHEESE PANCAKES-5 cakes, sour cream strawberry jam, sausage/bacon 4

on Sunday's only-EGGS BENEDICT-2 eggs poached, canadian bacon, hollandaise sauce on an english muffin 4.50

OMELETTE'S

includes toast and jelly
3 egg plain 2.50
3 egg cheese 3.00
3 egg MAGGIE'S SPECIAL-ham and cheese, your choice of mushrooms, onions, green peppers, tomatoes, sour cream 3.75

COMBO'S

1 egg, toast and jelly 1.25
2 eggs, toast and jelly 1.75
1 egg, sausage/bacon , toast and jelly 2.50
2 eggs, sausage/bacon, toast and jelly 3.00
2 eggs, ham, hash browns, toast and jelly 4.00
french toast (2) sausage/bacon 2.75
buckwheat cakes (5) sausage/bacon 2.75
2 muffins, 2 eggs, sausage/bacon 3.00
continental breakfast: english muffin, coffee/tea/milk and juice 2.25
calorie counter: ½ grapefruit, 1 egg, toast and jelly 2.25

ALA CARTE

1 egg, any style	.50
2 eggs, any style	1.00
toast and jelly	.85
cereal, toast and jelly	1.85
bagel and cream cheese	1.10
cinnamon or caramel roll	.85
english muffin	.95
homemade muffin of the day	.85
buckwheats (5)	1.60
buckwheats (3)	1.35

ALA CARTE

french toast (3)
french toast (2)
sausage/bacon
ham
hash browns/ american fries
½ grapefruit
cantaloupe (in season)
yogurt
peanut butter
jack gunderson's maple syrup

BEVERAGES

coffee	.50
decafe	.60
tea	.45
flavored tea	.60
cocoa	.50
small milk	.50
large milk	1.00
small juice	.75
large juice	1.00

BISCUIT MENU

biscuit and butter
biscuit and butter, cheese
add on:
tomato, onion or lettuce
egg or turkey
sausage or bacon

Maggie's Lunch
11:30 am - 4 p.m.

APPETIZERS

FRENCH FRIES 1.00
GERMAN FRIES 1.00
HOMEMADE CHIPS 1.00
CLASSIC CHIPS 1.00

ONION RINGS 2.00
WHITEFISH LIVERS [illegible] 2.50
CHICKEN WINGS 1.25
sweet & sour or barbecue 1.50

MAGGIE'S INTERNATIONAL BURGERS

USA EAST 3.50
hamburger, french fries, pickle
with cheese .25 extra

CANADIAN BURGER 4.00
canadian bacon, swiss cheese on a beef pattie, french fries

MEXICAN BURGER 3.75
cheese and refried beans on a beef pattie, topped with hot sauce and sour cream, taco chips

CIA BURGER 4.00
swiss, colby, blue cheese or cheddar cheese, inside a beef pattie, french fries

ITALIAN BURGER 3.75
pizza sauce, pepperoni, mozarella cheese on a beef pattie, homemade chips

FRENCH BURGER 3.75
mushrooms, red onion and blue cheese on a beef pattie, french fries

USA WEST 4.00
california burger, french fries, pickle
with cheese .25 extra

GERMAN BURGER 3.75
homemade sauerkraut on a beef pattie, pickle, german fries

GREEK BURGER 3.75
marinated black olives, onion, cherry tomatoes, feta cheese on a beef pattie, served on pita bread

IRISH BURGER 4.25
corned beef, cheddar cheese on a beef pattie, horseradish sauce, classic chips

DANISH BURGER 4.00
shredded pot roast in beer, horseradish sauce, classic chips, pickle

ENGLISH BURGER 4.00
fresh Lake Superior whitefish or trout, deepfried, on a bun, homemade chips

BURGERS

HAMBURGER 2.50
CHEESEBURGER 2.75
CALIFORNIA BURGER 3.00
CALIFORNIA CHEESEBURGER 3.25
all burgers served with potato chips pickle

'WICHES

GRILLED CHEESE 1.75
GRILLED HAM AND CHEESE 2.50
HAM OR TURKEY 2.25
served with your choice of white, whole wheat or rye bread, potato chips, pickle
Pastrami on sourdough bread 2.75
served with potato chips pickle

SALADS

TOSSED GARDEN SALAD 1.25
MAGGIE'S CHEF SALAD 4.00
ITALIAN VEGETABLE SALAD 2.00
GREEK SALAD 3.50
FRUIT SALAD 4.00
PASTA SALAD 4.50
italian or french dressing included
1000 island .50 blue cheese .75
Creamy cucumber .75

BISCUITS

BISCUIT AND BUTTER .60
BISCUIT, BUTTER AND CHEESE .80
ADD ON:
TOMATO, ONION OR LETTUCE .35
EGG OR TURKEY .60
SAUSAGE OR BACON .80

Can we talk...
Our esteemed and world famous flamingo chef wishes to remind you that [illegible] our burger [illegible] from fresh [illegible] ground beef. The soups are made from scratch and Eunie makes the best pies in the world! Check the blackboard for daily specials and your dessert selections
substitutions 75 extra

PIZZA (after 4:00 p.m.)

Cheese
- Extra cheese, add
- Onions, celery, tomato, bell pepper, jalapenos, black or green olives, add
- Italian sausage, pepperoni, ground beef, fresh mushrooms or bacon

Maggies House Special - green olives, green peppers, celery, onions, choice of pepperoni, or Italian sausage

Paula's Favorite - pepperoni, sausage, mushrooms, black or green olives

Domestic Beers ---------- 1.75
Budweiser and Bud Light
Leinenkugel
Old Milwaukee
Old Style
Miller Genuine Draft
Miller Lite
Michelob, Michelob Light
Special Export, Export Light
Killian's Red Ale
Rolling Rock
Coors Light

Super Premium Beers
Summit Pale Ale ---------- 2.25
Leinenkugel Limited,Red ---------- 2.00
Anchor Steam and Porter ---------- 3.00

On Tap
1919 Draft Rootbeer.......... 1.00
Leinenkugel.......... 1.00
Bass Ale.......... 2.50

Non Alcoholic Beers
Sharps ---------- 1.75
O'Doul's ---------- 1.75
Kaliber ---------- 2.25

Pop and Mineral Water
Coke, Diet Coke, Sprite,Club Soda ---------- 1.00
Orange, Diet Sprite, Ginger Ale, Squirt ---------- 1.00
Buddies Orange ---------- 1.25
LaCroix Mineral Water ---------- 1.00
Fruit Juice Sparklers ---------- 1.50
Lemonade ---------- 1.00
Hot Bayfield Apple Cider ---------- 1.00

MAGGIE'S RED WINE RACK

	glass	bottle
92 Jean Marc Aujoux *Beaujolais-Vill*	3.50	13.00
91 Bogle *Petite Sirah*	3.50	13.00
90 Napa Ridge *Merlot*	3.50	13.00
90 Fetzer *Barrel Select Zinfandel*	3.50	13.00
90 Kendall Jackson *Zinfandel*	3.50	13.00

Australia
Fosters giant can
Canada
LaBatt's Blue
Molson Golden
Moosehead
Czechoslovakia
Pilsner Urquel
Denmark
Carlsberg Elephant
England
Bass Ale
Watney's Red Barrel
Germany
Beck's Light and Dark
St. Pauli Light and Dark
Hacker Pschorr Weiss
Holland
Amstel
Grolsch 16 ounce
Heineken
Ireland
Guiness Stout
Harp Lager
Mexico
Corona Extra
Dos Equis

MAGGIE'S WHITE WINE RAC

	glass
92 Beringer *White Zinfandel*	3.00
91 Parker *Johannisberg Riesling*	3.50
92 Mitchelton *Marsanne*	3.50
91 Murphy Goode *Fume Blanc*	3.50
91 Napa Ridge *Chardonnay*	3.25

Bartles and Jaymes Wine Cooler
Jug Wine - Chablis or Rhine

Rum and Bayfield cider ---------- 2.75

Have a great Apple Fest!

Apple fest '93 Menu

"starters"

French fries or homemade chips.......... 1.50
Toasted baquette with whole roasted garlic.......... 2.50
Black beans and rice.......... 3.25
Flamingo tenders.....buffalo style.......... 3.95

"char-broiled burgers"

Canadian Burger......canadian bacon and swiss cheese.......... 4.25
Plain Ol' Burger......3.25......with cheese......3.75......make it a california.......... 4.25
Mushroom Swiss Burger......just what it says folks.......... 4.25
All American Burger......bacon cheeseburger.......... 4.25
French Burger......sauteed mushrooms, red onion and blue cheese.......... 4.25
Blackened Burger......with cajun spices, tomato and our secret sauce.......... 4.25

"almost burgers"

Danish Burger.....shredded pot roast, baked in beer with horseradish sauce.......... 4.50
Maggies Superior Sandwich.....fresh lake trout or whitefish, pan fried.......... 4.75
Grilled Chicken Breast.....southwestern, cajun or BBQ style.......... 4.75

"soups"

Maggies chili.......... 2.50
check the board for dailies

"salads"

Tossed garden salad.......... 2.50.......... **Italian veggie salad**.......... 2.50
(with Maggies homemade french, italian,blue cheese or ranch dressing)

"desserts"

check the board for apple fest delights
no separate checks or substituitions please

check the board for Maggies dinner favorites starting at 4:30 p.m.

WAITRESSES

Arrive at work 15 minutes prior to scheduled time, dressed, neat &
checking your work area for readiness.

TABLE IS SET PROPERLY 6.

A. Silverware is stocked, clean.
B. Napkins and Placemats are in order and placed accurately on tabl
C. Salt and pepper shakers, sugar bowl is clean and filled.
D. Clean ashtray on the table, 2 for double tables.
E. Chairs & tables are relatively neat and orderly.
F. Flowers are fresh and watered.

SET UP SERVICE AREA

A. Dressings are filled.
B. Ketchup and Mustard are filled.
C. Jams and jellys filled and wiped clean.
D. Syrup pitchers are filled and clean.
E. Coffee filters filled. Yogurt & Cereals supplied
F. Desserts sliced and covered in refrig.
G. Soups are adequately filled in warmer. Check for freshness
H. Blackboards are written and current.

Check with cooks for daily specials, items that are out, etc. Know
on the menu, how it is made, prepared, etc.

All customers must be treated with courtesy, respect, friendliness a
smile on your face. This is expected of you!

At the end of your shift leave it as you would want to find it. Re
replace, wipe clean and wash laundry. Report to the cook any item
you know we are about out of, or out of completely. Never leave yo
until you are satisfied the next waitress is adequately prepared to
Never leave anything empty.

Always keep your eyes moving over the dining room. There are alway
cups to be filled, plates to be cleared, second drinks orders to be

For tables who want separate checks, ma
tickets so the cooks know which orders a
sitting together and need to be served at t
time. A system that should work is star
with A mark your tickets A 1, A 2, A 3 a
equal the number of people the next separate
check order B-1, B 2 etc.

Maggies Breakfast

6am-11am

Fisherman's Special - 2 eggs, sausage/bacon, hash browns, toast and jelly 4.50

Logger's Special - 3 buckwheats, 2 eggs, sausage/bacon 4.00

Huevos Rancheros - flour tortilla, refried beans, 2 eggs, Colby cheese, sauce, sour cream 3.50

Omelettes - includes toast and jelly
- 3 egg plain 2.75
- 3 egg cheese 3.25
- 3 egg Maggies Special - ham and cheese, your choice of mushrooms, onions, green peppers, tomatos, sour cream 4.75

Ala Carte

- 1 egg, any style .60
- 2 eggs, any style 1.20
- toast and jelly .95
- Cereal, toast and jelly 1.95
- bagel and cream cheese 1.20
- Cinnamon or Caramel Roll .95
- English Muffin 1.05
- homemade muffin of the day .95
- buckwheats (5) 1.70
- buckwheats (3) 1.45

Ala Carte

- french toast 1.95
- french toast 1.70
- sausage/bacon 1.45
- ham 1.70
- hash browns/American fries 1.20
- ½ grapefruit 1.20
- ½ cantaloupe 1.70
- Yogurt 1.00
- peanut butter .60
- Jack Gunderson's maple syrup .60

Beverages

- Coffee .60
- decafe .75
- tea .50
- iced tea .50
- Cocoa .60
- Milk .65 1.15
- juices 1.25 1.95

Biscuit Menu

- Biscuit and butter
- Biscuit butter and cheese .80
- add on:
- tomato onion or lettuce .35
- egg or turkey .60
- sausage or bacon .80

Check the Blackboard for the features of the menu!
substitutions .75 extra
No ½ orders please

THE PERFECT BEGINNING

MAGGIE'S

NEW YEAR'S EVE DINNER

DECEMBER 31, 1990
6PM - 10PM

Prime Rib or Shrimp Scampi

Wild Rice Soup or Salad

Potatoes and Fresh Vegetable

A Glass of Champagne, Dessert & Coffee

12.95

Not to Mention a Free Drink at Morty's Pub to Ring in the New Year

Above: Janel Ryan and Junior Yeska who owned Juniors before it became Maggie's

New Year's Eve Menu

Sunday, December 31, 2017
5:00 pm - 8:00 pm
$45.00 per person

FIRST COURSE

Mixed brassica salad, cider vinaigrette,
sweet kuri squash puree, seeds & nuts

MAIN COURSE

Braised beef short rib,
happy hollow cheesy polenta,
citrus season gremolata

DESSERT

Croissant pudding, egg nog anglaise,
kumquat compote

New Year's Eve Menu

Wednesday, December 31, 2014
5:00 pm - 8:00 pm
$45.00 per person

Glass of Prosecco

FIRST COURSE

Caribbean Shrimp Stuffed Potato Skins
jalapeño pepper, pineapple, tomatoes, limes,
cilantro, feta cheese

SECOND COURSE

Chilled Butter Poached Lobster Salad
bibb lettuce, crispy pork belly, red onion, craisins,
champagne, mango dressing

THIRD COURSE

Poutine Maggie's Style
pan seared foie gras, match sticks fries, cheese curds,
caramelized onion sauce

FOURTH COURSE

Duel Beef Sliders
Grilled Beef Tenderloin
aged white cheddar, sautéed mushrooms, onions
Bacon Burger
Happy Hollow sheep's milk cheese, side of sauteed spinach
and white beans, giardiniera vegetables

FIFTH COURSE

Crêpe
vanilla cream filled, chocolate, banana sauce

The people make it happen

Upper left: Laura (mother of Linda Jorgenson), ,Jack Gunderson, Linda Jorgenson

Above: Halversons

Upper right: Annie and Ray Howe

Left: Irene (Sharon Wszalek's mother), Dick Radke, Wilmer (Red) and Ruthann Compton

Lower left: Doty Compton, Mary Lampa

Below: Chad Defoe

Right: Marian Jonis

Above: Sharon Dahl
Right: Hadland

Above: Randy Anderson, Nick Lund, Jim Webster
Below: Mary Rice and John Spencer dressed as "favorite tourists"

Back row, l-r: Kat Simmons, Courtney Dugger, Kaite Sweval Bartyn, Ivy Stelmaszewski Meierotto, Nancy Erickson
Front row, l-r: Hayley Webster, Shannon Anderson, Mary Rice

At left: Amy Hanson French and Colleen Kinney, probably taken at the "come as your favorite tourist" party at Bates mid to late '80s

The people make it happen

GO FOR IT!

Mary was a great person who touched so many people with her positive attitude and enormous generosity.

I was a young man who came to her in 1985 with an idea to start a music camp on Madeline Island even though I had no experience running a music camp. She liked the idea, said, "Go for it!" and became the founding benefactress—an angel for Madeline Island Music Camp. With her and her family's financial support she helped me attain a career I could never have imagined at the time. Thousands of young aspiring musicians benefited over the years.

She had an outrageous sense of humor. During a formal fundraising event and dinner she made us all laugh when she came over to our table while we were eating our fancy, gourmet dinner and **brought over a plate of White Castle hamburgers with mustard and ketchup on the side**!

I miss her and will remember her as one of the most important people in my life.

—Thomas George

Grandon and Dot Harris

Stephanie and Ellie Bresette

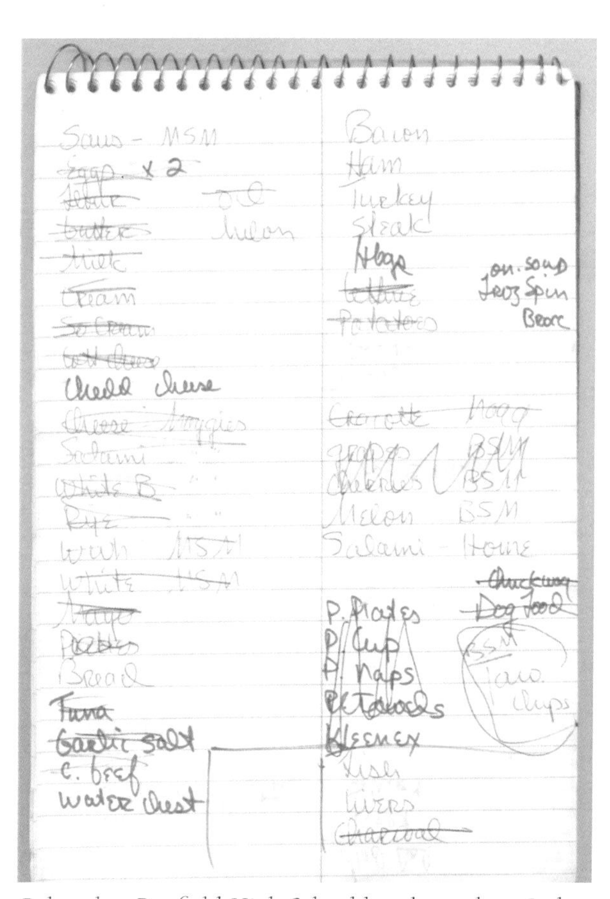

Below, l-r: Bayfield High School band members Josh Pearson, Graham Went, Ted Galazen, Tyler Heckman, Lucas DePerry

Below right: Dave Pierpont

KID-FRIENDLY PLACE

It's so great to write about Maggie's and Mary Rice! I am originally from Minneapolis, have been vacationing in Bayfield for about 30 years and about four years ago, moved here permanently. I have known Mary, Molly, and Katherine for years. I was first introduced to Mary about 13 years ago by a mutual Minneapolis friend, her hairdresser Will O'Hara. My family had many dinners at Maggie's and Wild Rice and at Mary's home. In the winter Maggie's was so special, catering to the locals.

Maggie's was always the dependable, fun place to go where you knew the staff and customers. Mary came in with friends and family and usually sat at the back, right hand tables. I always loved Applefest with Mary and her entourage decorated in pink flamingos; this is what Bayfield was about. Mary was such a genuine person; she would always stop and talk with me and check on the family. She helped Bayfield so much! Her generosity has meant so much to so many.

Maggie's was a kid-friendly place. Half-priced Wednesday burger nights were awesome. Deserts, drinks, people, and staff were great! Mary is missed by all and Maggie's will be missed too; it was a Bayfield icon.

—*Wendy Cariveau*

Wendy Cariveau, Annalisa Bermel, Teigan Bermel

Above: Hayley Webster
Below Paul and Joyce Bratti

The people make it happen

L-r: Barbara McFarland, Sara Muender, Karlyn Holman, Karen Thiel, France Austin Miller

ICE CREAM, MARGARITAS, CHOCOLATE

Wish I had taken photos at the many happy events, evenings, meals at Maggie's; too many photo ops!

Fond memories of being with Mary were meals that Dale and Louie would make special when Mary traveled to Italy or on her return. They treated her like the Queen we loved and admired.

The theme of Maggie's will be remembered in my heart as friends old and new, family, celebrations including my 60th birthday and Mary's 70th. At her big event under the flamingo tent were friends and family, some from the Bahamas. Most favorite taste treats of all included ice cream, margaritas, and all things chocolate.

Gatherings at Mary's "special table" were also made special with guests/friends/family who would swop stories, highlights from any given day, or memories of days past. As Mary would say, "It was "never boring."

Many times Harvey noticed folks at other tables watching the fun and made an introduction, after conversation, asking if they would like to meet "Maggie" who was always pleased to meet and greet others. She would often make a tour to chat with friends also enjoying the evening, especially true on Winter Burger Nites ... half price and special offerings.

The photos from so many places and events past were a treat, including one taken on a road tour with Mary to Madeline Island—the Hulings' property name sign. So many people offered and Mary accepted photos special to them, always with a stories. Almost annually, Mary rearranged, for better placement, the art and memorabilia on the walls. Most often bar pics would stay the same, especially one of John Hanson, often Mary's guest at dinner.

One more memory was not at Maggie's, but with Tiny as our driver after Maggie's closed, we all jumped in Mary's Mercedes to take a trip on the ice road and pop a bottle of champagne half way home. It may have even been after a New Year's Eve at Maggie's.

So many heart-filled moments. So many people would say the same.

—Janet and Harvey

WHAT DO PEOPLE DO AROUND HERE?

In the 1990s, a travel video production crew was in Bayfield for a couple of days to film a half hour show for broadcast in the U.K. I met with them to give some additional ideas for their show.

They were interested in stories about quirky local people. I told them the story of a waitress from Juniors.

One day, a table of tourists asked, "What the hell do people do around here?" She responded "**We fish, we fuck, and we drink.**" Their next question was, "What do you do in the winter?" Her immediate response was, "We don't fish so much."

The video crew loved the story so much that they filmed Heidi Nelson and me sitting at Maggie's bar as Heidi told the tale.

So, somewhere in British TV travel show files, there is a little bit of Juniors and Maggie's.

—Larry McDonald (Bayfield mayor, 1994-2004 and 2006-2016)

More reasons to celebrate!

Maggie's Happy 30th Birthday Celebration!

Maggie's Free-For-All

There is no Free Lunch, However

Dinner is Free all Night

Sunday October 27th 5pm - 9pm

Enjoy a Buffet Style Dinner on us

Say Hello to the Friends you, and we,

haven't seen all summer.

Thanks for all Your Support this Summer!

Maggie's Fall & Winter Hours

Starting Oct. 26th
Breakfast on Sat. & Sun. Only
Coffee at 6am Breakfast at 7am
Lunch & Dinner Daily
Open at 11am

The people make it happen

FIRST TIME I MET MARY

Back in the day, probably my second year at Morty's, I came in on an off day to check things. When I unlocked the door, Heidi, Chris, and Mary were having a meeting by the pool table. I apologized for intruding and left promptly. **That moment was the first time I had ever seen Mary.** I was intimidated and left scared—like I had made a big boo boo but I was reassured that I knew Heidi already, and she liked me! I will never forget that Heidi gave me confidence that everything was cool.

—from a FB page, from Nick Lunde to Heidi

A TYPICAL DAY

Clock in at 4:00 p.m. as day bartender means finishing stocking the bar with booze, changing kegs, making sure fruit garnish is prepped, closing bar tabs, etc. All good and ready to go!

People start trickling in 5:00 p.m. or so: locals picking up to-go orders; light conversation with bar guests who want to know what Bayfield is all about; and exchanging contact info with tourists I have bonded with (I can visit them in their own bars on my day off and they even offer houses for me to stay at!).

The Fun Time

6:00 p.m. or so: The "trickle" of people has morphed into a steady flow. Guests are being seated, drink order tickets being taken care of, and guests at the deck window order appetizers while they wait for a table. Me: discreetly escaping to the private wait station area to chomp on the burger I ordered.

6:30 p.m. or so: shit hits the fan! The bar and restaurant are full, there is a line out the door, deck is overflowing with a clogged bar window, and drink order tickets for dining room are piling up, When I pick up the phone, they can't understand why we don't take reservations and want me to recite the entire menu. The keg goes dry and needs changing, I'm out of ice, servers are running round like chickens without heads and at the same time seeing to my needs and me to theirs. This is a normal summer night. Imagine all this chaos. When the unexpected happens, the internet goes down and we have no credit card processing. Power outage. Short staffed. Murphy's Law!

10:00 p.m.: The carnage is over and I am winding down with a drink, sharing battle stories with fellow workers. Breathe …

11:00 p.m.: I am in my car heading home exhausted but with a pocket full of tips, smiling and ready to do it all again the next day!

11:15 p.m. Halfway home to Washburn I just realized I did not finish my burger. It was still there in the wait station, half eaten.

—Nick Lunde

Lois ("Louie") Stensvad

25 FLAMINGO FACTS or FALLACIES

Flamingos migrate to Wisconsin in December.
Ancient Egyptians revered the flamingo as a living symbol of the sun God Ra.
They considered flamingo tongue a delicacy.
Leominster Massachusetts is home of the world famous "pink lawn flamingo."
Check out their website; www.unionproducts.com
Flamingos are found in tropical and sub-tropical areas as well as Bayfield, WI.
Flamingos are very sophisticated and are noted for their refined taste in music as well as wine.
The correct term for a flock of flamingos is a pat of flamingos.
The Flamingo Hilton in Las Vegas was built by infamous mobster Bugsy Siegel.
(What's up with that quip)?
There are five species of flamingos.
A flamingos pink color comes from a diet high in pink lemonade.
Flamingos are very social birds. Colonies of tens of thousands are common.
(Especially the first weekend in October).
Flamingos have 12 to 25 tail feathers.
The word flamingo is derived from the Latin flamma, or Greek flame.
In 1957 the phoenicoptertis rubber plasticus (pink flamingo lawn ornament)
burst on the American scene.
Fossilized flamingo footprints estimated to be seven million years old,
have been found in the Andes Mountains.
Flamingos are ubiquitous at Maggie's. The last count being 5,425.
The average life span of the flamingo is 25 years.
Mary H. Rice began the Pink Flamingo Club back in 1980.
The neck of the flamingo is sinuous and has 25 elongated vertebrae.
Flamingos sense of taste is poorly developed and they have little or no sense of smell.
Newly hatched flamingo chicks are grey or white. Juveniles are grayish also,
taking one to two years to obtain pink coloration.
Flamingos devote considerable time to collective displays
and are often seen doing the macarena.
(Check out our wait staff's rendition).
Flamingos have knees that bend backward.
However what we refer to as their knee is actually their ankle.
The Andean flamingo is the only species of flamingo to have yellow legs and feet.
The "pink flamingo" is a signature drink at Maggie's.
(Ask your server for one of these tasty concoctions).
Lastly, the flamingo decor at Maggie's is not for sale
so PLEASE! No crying, begging, whining, or bartering.
However... the T-shirts are for sale!
(Ask your server for sizes and colors available).

"Help Maggie's flamingo bird find her way home!"

After hours

Have you batched out? Get back and put it in the bag!

Where's the "Z" tape? Is it in the bag??????

Reminders for bartenders and servers before clocking out of shift and depositing individual money bags to be dropped at Bremer Bank nightly.

Drayk Hoopman

V Ruiz and Mary Kay Defoe taking lemon drop birthday shots! (V is her nickname; it's really Valencia.) Lower far left: Hayley Webster

SOUPS AND CHILIS

French Onion Soup

- 8 large onions, julienned
- 1 bay leaf
- 1 Tbsp dried thyme
- ½ Lb. butter
- 1 Tsp. chopped garlic
- 1 ½ Cups sherry
- 2 Cans beef broth
- 1 Can chicken broth
- Salt and white pepper

Heat butter in braiser pan until brown. Add

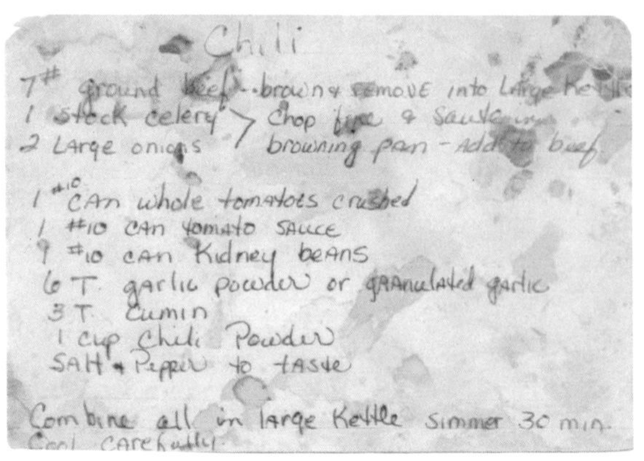

Chili
7# ground beef - brown & remove into large kettle
1 stock celery } chop fine & saute in browning pan - Add to beef
2 Large onions
1 #10 Can whole tomatoes crushed
1 #10 can tomato sauce
1 #10 can Kidney beans
6 T. garlic powder or granulated garlic
3 T. Cumin
1 cup Chili Powder
Salt & Pepper to taste

Combine all in large kettle simmer 30 min.
Cool carefully

onions, bay leaf, thyme. Cook until onions carmelize to deep brown, stirring often. Add garlic and cook for 2 minutes. Add sherry and cook for 1 minute. Add stocks and simmer for 20 minutes. Skim top often. Salt and pepper to taste.

Maggie's Chili

- 7 Lbs. ground beef
- 1 bunch celery
- 2 large yellow onions
- 10 Lbs. Can whole tomatoes, crushed
- 10 Lbs. Can tomato sauce
- 1 Cup regular chili powder (not Tex-mex)
- 6 Tbsp. garlic powder
- 3 Tbsp. cumin powder
- 1 Tbsp. salt
- 2 Tsp. black pepper
- 10 Lbs. Can kidney beans with juice

Brown ground beef in large sauté pan on high heat. There should be no excess juice or fat. Clean and finely chop celery and onion. Add to browned beef in large sauté pan and cook until tender. Crush whole tomatoes. Add tomatoes, sauce and spices to beef. Simmer together for 1 hour. Remove from heat. Add beans to chili and stir well. Chili cooks faster with the addi-

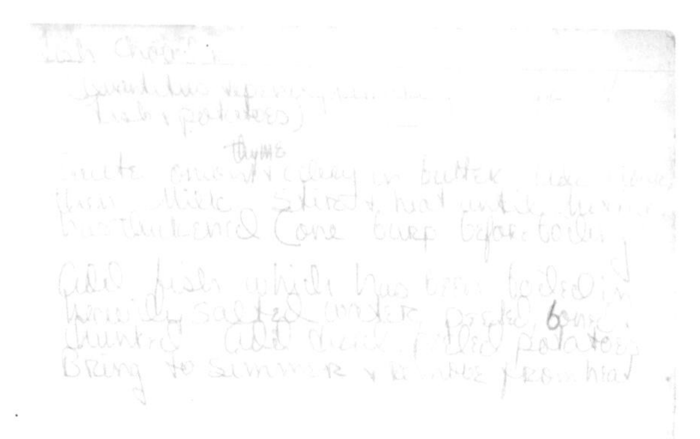

tion of cold beans. Stir to hasten cooling. Put in containers, label and date. Shelf life: 4 days refrigerated (Soup spoils when held at room temperature because of the kidney beans. Cool quickly after cooking, reheat thoroughly before serving.)

Black Bean Chili – Texas Chili

- 10 Cups raw black turtle beans, washed.
- 24 Cups cold water
- 4 Tsp. salt to taste

Combine beans, water, and salt. Bring to boil. Reduce heat and simmer covered until the beans are soft but not mushy. Beans and water should measure about 9 Cups when finished. The beans should have a slightly thick "gravy" appearance.
Set aside in kettle.

- 7 Lbs. chuck roast
- 2 Tbsp. corn oil
- 1 Tbsp. corn oil if needed

Quickly trim and cut meat into 1/2" cubes. Sauté meat in 1 Tbsp. oil until very brown. Take each batch out and reserve until all are finished. Put all batches back in sauté pan.

- 6 Cups water

Put water into the sauté pan with the meat and place in oven at 350 until meat is soft and tender. About 1 ½ hours. Meat and juice should equal 6 Cups.

- 6 Cups onions (pizza-size dice)
- 1 ½ green pepper (pizza-size dice)
- 16 finely diced garlic cloves
- 2 Tbsp. corn oil
- 1 Tbsp. corn oil if needed

Sauté veggies in oil over high heat until soft. Use more oil if necessary. When everything is cooked, add meat and veggies to bean kettle. Deglaze meat pan with water and add to beans.

Fish Chowder

- 12 potatoes, white, peeled

Wash and peel potatoes. Boil until tender. Cool. Dice potatoes into ¼ inch pieces. Reserve.

- 4 Lbs. whitefish or trout fillets

Cover and poach fish in microwave until tender. Cool, skin, remove bones and break into chunks. Reserve.

- 8 Oz. butter, melted
- 2 Cups flour, white

Melt butter in large kettle. Add flour. Mix until smooth

- 2 onions, ¼ inch chopped
- 1 bunch celery ¼ inch chopped

Add onions and celery to roux. Sauté until transparent.

- 3 Qt. milk, whole
- 2 Pt. half and half
- 1 Tbsp. thyme leaf

Add milk, half and half and thyme to roux. Bring cram sauce to a simmer. Cook until thick, whisking often until mixture bubbles in the center. DO NOT BOIL. Remove from heat

- Salt and pepper to taste

Add cold fish and potatoes (helps to cool soup faster). Season to taste with salt and pepper. Divide soup into smaller containers to cool. Stir frequently to cool more rapidly. Cover, label, date and refrigerate until needed.

Mushroom Soup

- 3 Lbs. mushrooms, sliced
- 1 Cup butter
- 1 Cup flour
- 1 Gallon milk
- Salt and pepper to taste

Sauté mushrooms in butter. Add flour and mix well. Add milk and mix well, bring to simmer Wait for one "burp" just before boiling.

SAUCES/DRESSINGS

Apostle (1,000) Island Dressing

- 4 Cup mayo
- 1 Cup sweet relish
- ½ Cup ketchup
- 3 hard boiled eggs, chopped fine

Combine well and store in covered container.

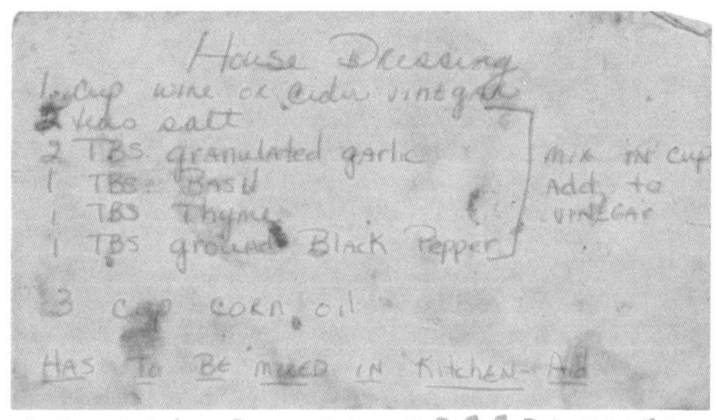

House Dressing
1 Cup wine or cider vinegar
2 TBS granulated garlic
1 TBS Basil
1 TBS Thyme
1 TBS ground Black Pepper
mix in cup Add to vinegar
3 cup corn oil
HAS TO BE MIXED IN KITCHEN-AID

1 Lb. Butter
1/4t ~~1/2t.~~ Cayenne Pepper

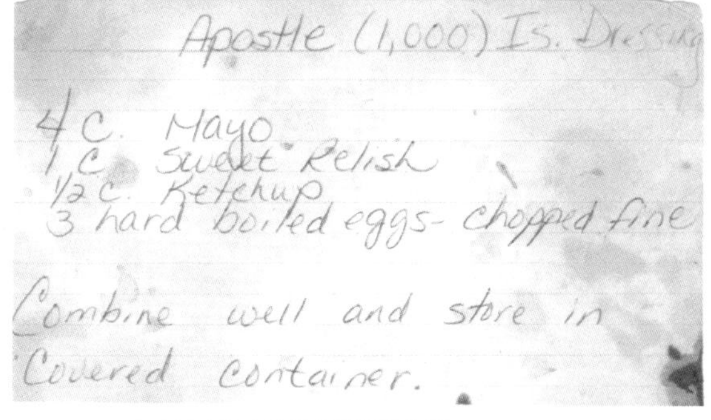

Apostle (1,000) Is. Dressing
4 C. Mayo
1 C. Sweet Relish
1/2 C. Ketchup
3 hard boiled eggs - chopped fine
Combine well and store in Covered container.

Recipes

Flamingo Tender Sauce

- 1 Lb. butter
- 4 Cups Durkees Red Hot Cayenne Sauce
- 1 Tbsp. Cajun seasoning
- ¼ Tsp. Cayenne pepper

Heat thoroughly in saucepan.

House Dressing

- 1 Cup wine or cider vinegar
- 2 Tsp. salt
- 2 Tbsp. granulated garlic
- 1 Tbsp. basil
- 1 Tbsp. thyme
- 1 Tbsp. ground black pepper

Mix ingredients and add to 3 Cups corn oil.
Has to be mixed in KitchenAid

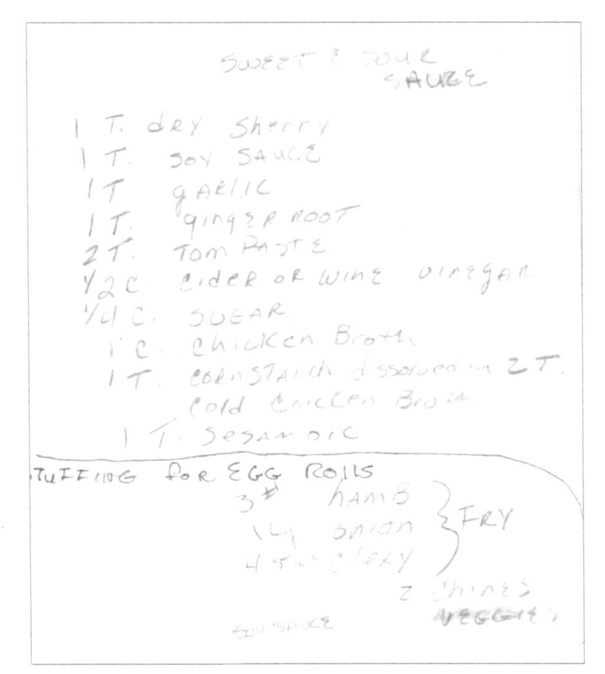

SWEET & SOUR SAUCE

1 T. dry Sherry
1 T. SOY SAUCE
1 T GARLIC
1 T. ginger ROOT
2 T. Tom PASTE
1/2 C. cider OR Wine vinegar
1/4 C. SUGAR
1 C. chicken Broth
1 T. CORNSTARCH dissolved in 2 T. cold chicken Broth
1 T. Sesame oil

STUFFING for EGG Rolls
3# hamB } FRY
1/4 onion
4 [illegible] celery
2 Chinese VEGGIES
SOY SAUCE

Secret Sauce

- 1 Gallon mayo
- 2- 5 Lb. sour cream
- 4 Tbsp. garlic salt
- 4 Tsp. celery salt
- 4 Tsp. cayenne pepper
- 3 Tbsp. paprika
- 3 Tbsp. onion powder
- 3 Tbsp. Worcheshire sauce
- 2 Tsp. curry powder
- 1 Tbsp. dill weed
- 1 Cup chives
- ¾ Cup white vinegar
- Juice of 2 lemons (or 4Tbsp. lemon juice)

Mix everything in large bowl.

Maggie's Cumin BBQ Sauce

- 20 Cups ketchup
- 5 Cups Worcestershire Sauce
- 2 Cups balsamic vinegar
- 3 Cups molasses
- 3 Cups Dijon mustard
- 6 Tbsp. Tabasco
- 4 Cups Red Hot sauce
- 12 Cups beef stock

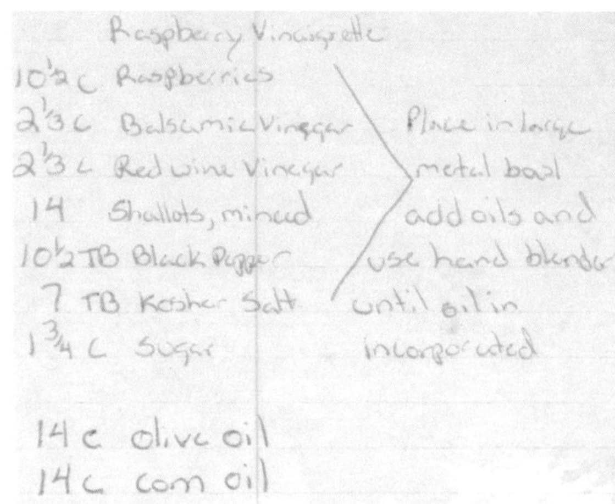

Raspberry Vinaigrette

10½ C Raspberries
2⅓ C Balsamic Vinegar
2⅓ C Red wine Vinegar
14 Shallots, minced
10½ TB Black Pepper
7 TB Kosher Salt
1¾ C Sugar

Place in large metal bowl add oils and use hand blender until oil in incorporated

14 c olive oil
14 c corn oil

Chicken Fajita Marinade

24 cups Corn Oil -
10 cups Lime Juice -
2 cups ground garlic -
1½ cups. Cumin -
1½ cups Oregano
2 TBSP Cayenne pepper -
2 oz Salt
3 cups Chopped Cilantro

- 1 Cup lime juice
- 1 Cup soy sauce
- ¾ Cup cumin
- ¼ Cup ground black pepper
- ¼ Cup coriander seed (ground)
- 8 Cups onions, chopped
- ¾ Cup garlic minced
- ¾ Cup jalapeno minced

Place ingredients in pot. Simmer 1 hour. Take off heat, cool. Run through bar mixer and strain.

Tartar Sauce

- ½ Gallon mayo
- ¼ Gallon pickle relish
- ½ Cup lemon juice
- 2 Tbsp. Worcestershire Sauce
- 1 Tbsp. dill weed
- 1 Cup onion minced
- 2 dashes Tabasco

Place everything in bowl and mix well

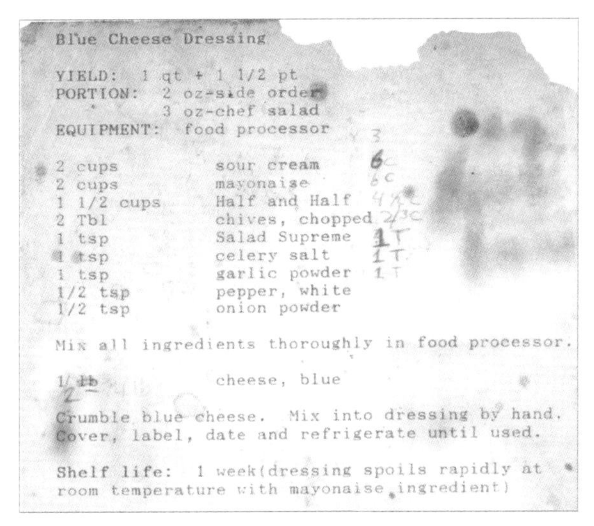

Blue Cheese Dressing

YIELD: 1 qt + 1 1/2 pt
PORTION: 2 oz-side order
3 oz-chef salad
EQUIPMENT: food processor

2 cups	sour cream
2 cups	mayonaise
1 1/2 cups	Half and Half
2 Tbl	chives, chopped
1 tsp	Salad Supreme
1 tsp	celery salt
1 tsp	garlic powder
1/2 tsp	pepper, white
1/2 tsp	onion powder

Mix all ingredients thoroughly in food processor.

1/ lb	cheese, blue

Crumble blue cheese. Mix into dressing by hand. Cover, label, date and refrigerate until used.

Shelf life: 1 week(dressing spoils rapidly at room temperature with mayonaise ingredient)

Tarragon Sauce

- ½ Gallon Mayo
- ½ Cup tarragon reduction
- 1 Tbsp. beef base dissolved in water
- 3 Tbsp. water
- ½ Cup tarragon vinegar

Pizza Sauce

- 10 Lbs. tomato sauce
- 1 Tbsp. oregano leaf
- 1 Tbsp. garlic powder
- 1 Tsp. onion powder
- ½ Tsp. black pepper
- ½ Tsp. salt

Combine tomato sauce with spices. Simmer for 30 minutes. Cool. Cover and refrigerate. Do not store in metal container or use tinfoil. Acid from tomatoes reacts with metal. Shelf life: 1 week

Blue Cheese Dressing

- 2 Cups sour cream
- 2 Cups mayonnaise
- 1 ½ Cups half and half
- 2 Tbsp. chopped chives
- 1 Tsp. salad supreme
- 1 Tsp. celery salt
- 1 Tsp. garlic powder
- ½ Tsp. white pepper
- ½ Tsp. onion powder

Mix ingredients thoroughly in food processor.

- ½ Lb blue cheese

Crumble blue cheese. Mix into dressing by hand. Cover, label, date, and refrigerate until used. Shelf life: 1 week

Ranch Dressing

- 6 Cups mayo
- 2 Cups buttermilk
- 1 Tsp. salt
- 1 Tsp. garlic powder
- 1 Tsp. onion powder
- ½ Tsp. salad seasoning
- 1 Tbsp. chives
- 1 Tbsp. lemon juice
- 2 dashes Tabasco
- ½ Tsp. curry powder
- 1/8 Tsp. allspice
- 1 Tbsp. dry mustard

Mix everything from above. Add herbs and blend until smooth.
Herbs: 1 Tbsp. green onion chopped, ½ Cup basil fresh, ½ Cup cilantro fresh, ½ Cup dill

French Dressing

- 10 Lbs. Can + 3 Cups ketchup
- 1 ½ Cups water
- 5 Cups corn oil
- 1 small onion, grated
- 7 ½ Cups sugar
- ½ Cup lemon juice
- 5 Cups cider vinegar
- 3 ½ Tbsp. celery salt
- 1 ½ Tbsp. paprika
- 1 ½ Tbsp. celery seed
- 1 ½ Tbsp. garlic powder

Mix together well in large pot. Put on stove at slow heat. NEVER BOIL Pull off heat, let cool.

Chicken Fajita Marinade

- 24 Cups corn oil
- 10 Cups lime juice
- 2 Cups ground garlic
- 1 ½ Cups cumin
- 1 ½ Cups oregano
- 2 Tbsp. cayenne pepper
- 2 Oz. salt
- 3 Cups chopped cilantro

Southwest Caesar Dressing

- ½ Tsp. ground cumin
- 2 ¼ Tsp. Dijon mustard
- 2 Heads roasted garlic
- ¼ Can chipotle chilies
- 4 each anchovy filet
- 2 Tbsp. balsamic vinegar
- ½ Cup lime juice
- 2 each shallots minced
- 2 Tbsp. cilantro
- 4 Oz egg yolks
- ½ Cup shredded parm
- ½ Tsp. salt
- ¼ Tsp cayenne pepper

In big Roboco put lime juice and chipotle peppers and blend well. Add everything in except the oils. Blend well. Add oils in slowly as the Roboco is on medium speed.

PASTA

Cold Noodle Hot Oil

- ½ Cup dry sherry
- ½ Cup white vinegar
- 1 Cup soy sauce
- ½ Cup granulated sugar
- ½ Cup sesame oil
- ¼ Cup Hot oil (chili oil)
- 6 cloves garlic, minced
- 2 heaping Tbsp. chopped ginger

Mix all together, taste. Add more hot oil if needed. Cook vermicelli or linguine. Immediately cool under cold water and drain.

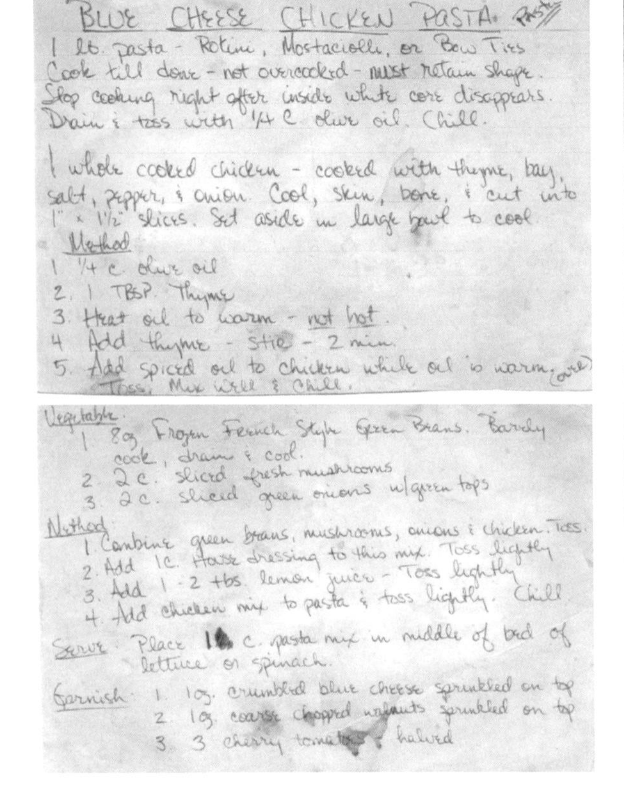

BLUE CHEESE CHICKEN PASTA.

1 lb. pasta - Rotini, Mostaciolli, or Bow Ties
Cook till done - not overcooked - must retain shape.
Stop cooking right after inside white core disappears.
Drain & toss with 1/4 C. olive oil. Chill.

1 whole cooked chicken - cooked with thyme, bay, salt, pepper, & onion. Cool, skin, bone, & cut into 1" x 1½" slices. Set aside in large bowl to cool

Method
1. 1/4 c. olive oil
2. 1 TBSP. Thyme
3. Heat oil to warm - not hot.
4. Add thyme - stir - 2 min.
5. Add spiced oil to chicken while oil is warm. Toss, Mix well & Chill.

Vegetable:
1. 8 oz Frozen French Style Green Beans. Barely cook, drain & cool.
2. 2 c. sliced fresh mushrooms
3. 2 c. sliced green onions w/green tops

Method
1. Combine green beans, mushrooms, onions & chicken. Toss.
2. Add 1C. House dressing to this mix. Toss lightly
3. Add 1-2 tbs. lemon juice - Toss lightly
4. Add chicken mix to pasta & toss lightly. Chill

Serve: Place 1 c. pasta mix in middle of bed of lettuce or spinach.

Garnish:
1. 1 oz. crumbled blue cheese sprinkled on top
2. 1 oz. coarse chopped walnuts sprinkled on top
3. 3 cherry tomatoes halved

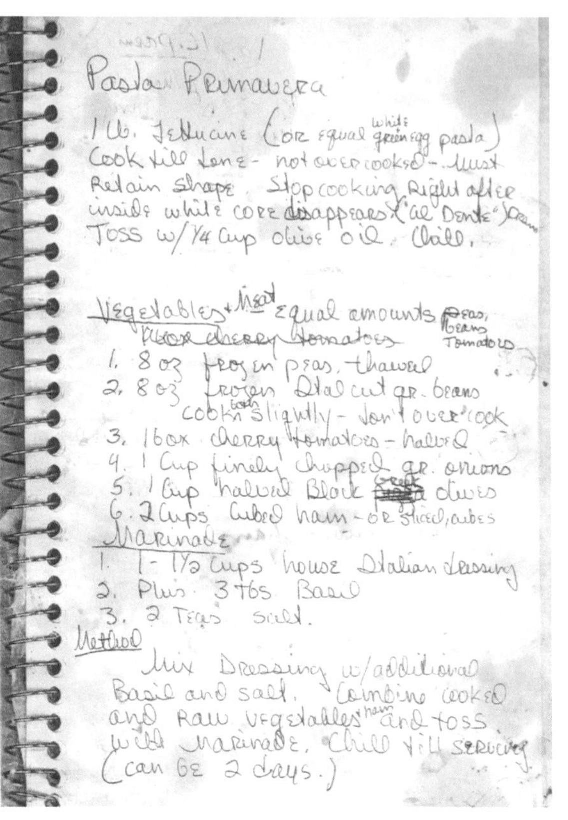

Pasta Primavera

1 Lb. Fettucine (or equal white green egg pasta)
Cook till done - not overcooked - Must Retain shape. Stop cooking right after inside white core disappears ("al Dente"). Toss w/ 1/4 Cup olive oil. Chill.

Vegetables + Meat - equal amounts peas, beans, tomatoes
1. 8 oz frozen peas, thawed
2. 8 oz frozen Ital cut gr. beans - cook both slightly - don't overcook
3. 1 box cherry tomatoes - halved
4. 1 Cup finely chopped gr. onions
5. 1 Cup halved Black olives
6. 2 Cups cubed ham - or sliced, cubes

Marinade
1. 1-1½ Cups house Italian dressing
2. Plus 3 Tbs Basil
3. 2 Teas salt.

Method
Mix Dressing w/additional Basil and salt. Combine cooked and raw vegetables + ham and toss with marinade. Chill till serving (can be 2 days.)

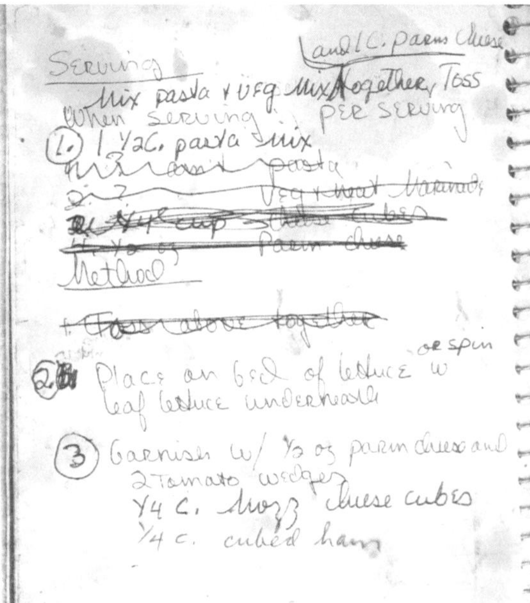

Serving
Mix pasta + veg. Mix together, Toss and 1C. parm cheese
When serving PER SERVING
1. 1 1/2 C. pasta mix

Method

2. Place on bed of lettuce or spin w leaf lettuce underneath
3. Garnish w/ 1/2 oz parm cheese and 2 Tomato wedges
1/4 C. Mozz cheese cubes
1/4 C. cubed ham

Place in bowl and pour sauce over. Marinate 2 hours. Place on spinach or other greens. Top with chopped scallions, slivered red bells or radish slices. Serve with roll and butter.

Blue Cheese Chicken Pasta

- 1 Lb. pasta–Rotini, Mostaciolli, or Bow Ties

Cook until done; not overcooked. Retain shape. Stop cooking right after inside white core disappears. Drain. Toss with ¼ Cup olive oil. Chill.

- 1 whole cooked chicken – cooked with thyme, bay leaf, salt, pepper and onion

Cool, skin, bone, and cut into 1"-1 ½" slices
Set aside in large bowl to cool.
Method:

- ¼ Cup olive oil
- 1 Tbsp. thyme

Heat oil to warm – not hot.
Add thyme – stir 2 minutes.
Add spiced oil to chicken while oil is warm.
Toss, mix well and chill

Vegetable:

- 8 Oz. frozen French style green beans: barely cook, drain, cool.
- 2 Cup sliced fresh mushroom.
- 2 Cup sliced green onions with green tops

Method: Combine green beans, mushrooms,

onions, and chicken, toss. Add 1 Cup house dressing to this mix. Toss lightly. Add 1-2 Tbsp. lemon juice. Toss lightly. Add chicken mix to pasta and toss lightly. Chill.

Serve: Place 1 Cup pasta mix in middle of bed or lettuce or spinach. Garnish: 1 Oz. crumbled blue cheese sprinkled on top; 1 Oz. coarse chopped walnuts sprinkled on top; 3 cherry tomatoes – halved

APPETIZERS

Polenta Fries

- 3 Cans chicken broth
- 1 Tbsp. fresh minced garlic
- 2 Tsp. black pepper
- 6 Cups cornmeal

Add the rest of the ingredients to broth. Stir until thicken and the cornmeal has cooked all the way. Corn is smooth. Place in sprayed half sheet pan. Let cool in the cooler until hardened.

Nachos

- Heaping 1/3 Cup of refried beans
- 1-2 handfuls tortilla chips
- 3 slices Jack cheese
- 3 slices Colby cheese

Put tortilla chips over ¾ of platter. Put refried beans on other ¼ end of the platter. Cover with 5 slices of cheese. Cover beans with 1 cheese slice. Zap in microwave until cheese melts.

Top with mixed green chopped onion and sliced black olives. Mix 1 cup at a time equally

- 2 heaping soup spoons onion/black olives
- 1 Oz. sour cream – top-middle of the nachos
- 3 Oz. salsa on side – choice of mild or hot

Best place to get whitefish livers which are one of my favorite foods. Always enjoyed taking groups of cousins there and giving them the chance to try that delicacy. Some of them had favorite drinks and always said Maggie's made them the best.

—Larry Reiten

Sautéed WhiteFish Livers

- 4 Oz. (1/3 Cup) livers coated with 1 Oz. cornmeal breading

Sauté in ½ Cup butter (oil or bacon grease optional) with 3-4 julienne green pepper strips, 1 slice onion, ¼ cup sliced mushrooms. Serve with 1 oz. tartar sauce in portion cup, 1 lemon wedge, 1 piece leaf lettuce

Deep Fried: • 4 Oz. (1/3 Cup) deep fried livers coated with 1 Oz. chicken wing breading

---

Food treats include livers, yummy sides and desserts. Roasted garlic added extra on pizza, burgers. Polenta fries were done "Mary's way". Every chef knew just what that meant.

—Janet and Harvey Sternat

BREAKFAST

Pumpkin Muffins

- ½ Cup pumpkin seeds

Toast pumpkin seeds over low heat in frying pan until crisp. Cool.

- 1 Cup whole milk
- ¾ Cup Canned pumpkin
- 1 egg
- ¼ Cup melted butter
- ½ Cup pumpkin seeds, toasted

Beat together milk, pumpkin, egg and butter. Add seeds and mix

- 2 Cups white flour
- 1 Cup brown sugar
- 2 Tsp. baking powder
- 2 Tsp. pumpkin pie spices
- ¼ Tsp. baking soda
- ¼ Tsp. salt

Sift together the dry ingredients. Make a well in the center and add the wet ingredients. Fold in with a rubber spatula, just until dry ingredients are moistened. Line muffin pan with paper liners. Scoop batter into 12 muffin cups. Bake in preheated 375 oven for 20-25 minutes or until golden brown. Test with a dry toothpick for doneness. Cool and cover until used.

Blueberry Pumpkin Muffins

- 1 2/3 Cups white flour
- ¼ Cup Millers Bran
- 1 Tsp. baking soda
- ½ Tsp. baking powder
- ½ Tsp. salt
- 1 Tsp. ground cinnamon
- ½ Tsp. ground allspice

Recipes

Sift together the dry ingredients. Reserve.

Streusel Topping
- 2 Tbsp. white flour
- 2 Tbsp. white sugar
- ¼ Tsp. cinnamon
- 1 Tbsp. butter

Combine flour, sugar and cinnamon in a small bowl. Cut in butter until crumbly. Reserve.
- 1 Cup solid pack pumpkin
- ¼ Cup evaporated milk, undiluted.

Combine pumpkin and milk in small bowl. Reserve.

- 1/3 Cup oil
- 1 Cup brown sugar (packed)

Cream oil and sugar. Add 1 egg to oil/sugar mix. Beat until fluffy. Add flour alternately with pumpkin mixture. Beat well after each addition.

- 1 Cup blueberries, frozen, cranberries, chopped or apples, peeled and finely diced
- 1 Tbsp. white flour

Combine fruit and flour. Fold into pumpkin batter. Line muffin pan. Scoop batter into 18 muffin cups. Sprinkle with streusel topping. 350 oven, 40 minutes. Test with toothpick.

Apple Streusel Muffin Batter

- 1 ½ Cups white flour
- ½ Cup white sugar
- ¼ Cup Miller's Bran
- 2 Tsp. baking powder
- 1 Tsp. ground cinnamon
- ¼ Tsp. ground allspice
- ¼ Tsp. baking soda
- Dash of salt

Combine flour, sugar and remaining dry ingredients and spices in large mixing bowl.

- 2 eggs
- 1 Cup sour cream
- ¼ Cup oil
- 1 Tsp. vanilla extract

Combine eggs, sour cream and oil in a separate bowl.

- 1 Cup apple, unpeeled, diced.

Add apples to egg mixture. Combine thoroughly. Pour egg mixture over flour mixture. Fold in with a rubber spatula, just until flour is moistened. Line muffin pan with paper liners. Scoop batter into 12 muffin cups. Top each muffin with about 2 Tsp. of streusel topping.

Streusel Topping

- ½ Cup walnuts, finely chopped
- ¼ Cup white flour
- 3 Tbsp. white sugar
- 2 Tbsp. butter or margarine, room temp
- ¼ Tsp. ground cinnamon

Mix above ingredients with a fork until mixture looks like small peas. Reserve.

S.O.S

- 2 hard boiled eggs

Cover eggs with cold water and bring to a simmer. Cook for 8-10 minutes or until hard boiled. Cool under running water. Reserve.

- 6 Tbsp. melted butter
- ½ Cup white flour

Melt butter in sauce pan. Add flour to make a roux. Beat until smooth.

- 4 Cups whole milk

Add milk to roux and stir until smooth. Simmer until cream sauce thickens and bubbles in the middle of the sauce.

- 1 Jar Armour dried beef 4 ½ Oz.
- ¼ Tsp. black pepper

Add beef and pepper to cream sauce. Dice egg and add. Cool, cover, and refrigerate until used.

Plate Presentation:
- 1 biscuit, split or 2 slices toast
- 1 Cup S.O.S.
- 1 fruit garnish

Cottage Cheese Pancakes

- 4 eggs, room temperature

Separate 4 eggs (room temp whites beat to a larger volume) Beat whites until soft peaks form. Reserve

- 1 ½ Cups white flour
- 1 Cup cottage cheese
- 4 egg yolks
- 4 Tbsp. butter melted
- 4 Tbsp. butter milk to moisten
- Dash of salt

Beat everything together but egg whites. Fold in beaten whites with spatula. Fry pancakes on greased griddle. 2 Oz. ladle per pancake.

Crepe Batter

Beat eggs until foamy in a food processor or wire whip

- 1 Cup whole milk
- 2 Cups white flour
- 4 eggs
- ¼ Cup vegetable oil

Add milk, flour and oil to eggs. Whip just until smooth. Heat 1 Tsp. butter in crepe pan until it bubbles. Add 2 Oz. ladle batter (1/4 Cup).

Swirl to cover bottom of pan. Turn quickly and brown for a few seconds. Slide out of pan. Cool and stack with paper between each.

Egg White Omelet

Vegetables for egg white omelet

- 1 Cup chopped onion
- 2 Cups sliced mushroom
- 2 Tbsp. corn oil

Sauté onions in 1 Tbsp. oil until lightly browned and almost transparent. Add mushrooms and sauté quickly. Use high heat.

- 1 Cup finely chopped broccoli
- 1 Cup finely chopped cauliflower
- ¼ Cup water
- ½ Tsp. salt

Add broccoli and cauliflower and fry about 1 minute. Mix well. Add water and salt. Mix. Cover and steam until still crunchy. Cool and use in flat pan. Store covered up to 2 days. Use 1/3 Cup cooked vegetables for each omelet.

- 1/3 Cup steamed vegetables

Heat veggies. Spray pan with Pam.

- 3 egg whites per omelet.

Beat egg whites with fork or whisk until frothy. Pour into heated 8" pan. Cook until solid

- 2 Oz. Mozzarella

Add heated veggies to half of omelet, cover with other half. Slide onto plate and cover with cheese. Zap in microwave or broil until cheese melts. Serve with toast, jelly and fruit garnish.

Buckwheat Cakes

Dry Mix:

- 8 Cups whole wheat flour
- 8 Cups white flour
- 5 Tbsp. baking powder
- 3 Tbsp. soda
- 3 Tbsp. sugar
- 2 Tbsp. salt

Batter, Small

- 1 Cup dry mix
- 2 whole eggs
- 1 ¼ Cup buttermilk
- ¼ Cup and 1 Tbsp. corn oil

Batter, Medium

- 2 Cups mix
- 4 whole eggs
- 2 ½ Cup buttermilk
- ½ Cup and 2 Tbsp. corn oil

Baking Powder Biscuit

- 8 Cup flour
- 5 Tbsp. baking powder
- 2 Tbsp. salt
- 5 eggs
- ½ Cup corn oil
- 3 Cup milk

Mix. Bake 350 for 15 minutes. Yield: 40

BURGERS

Canadian Burger

- 5 Oz. beef patty
- 1 Oz. slice Swiss cheese
- 1 Oz. slice Canadian bacon

Put burger on gas grill and cook until almost to desired doneness. Fry Canadian bacon. Butter and grill bun. Put cooked bacon on cooked hamburger. Add Swiss cheese and cover until cheese melts. Put on bun and serve with choice potato, pickle on leaf lettuce.

German Burger

- 8 Oz. butter
- 6 Tbsp. flour
- 1 yellow onion chopped

Melt butter in heavy pan and stir until brown. Add flour and continue to brown until color of light coffee. Add onion. Cook until transparent.

- 1 Can sauerkraut (2 cups) washed, drained
- 2 Tbsp. caraway seeds
- 1 Tbsp. brown sugar
- Water to cover

Add remaining ingredients to pan and simmer uncovered for 2 hours. Remove from heat, cool and bag in portions with label and date. Freeze until needed

Burger

- 5 Oz. burger patty
- 2 Tbsp. German Sauerkraut

Grill burger patty on gas grill until done. Butter and grill bun. Heat sauerkraut. Put burger on bun and top with sauerkraut. Serve with German fries, pickle on lettuce leaf.

German fries

Cut pre-cooked red potatoes with skins on into 1 to 1 ½ inch pieces. Fry in deep fryer until brown.

Irish Burger

- 1, 5-Oz. burger patty
- 1 slice cooked corn beef
- 1 Oz. cheddar cheese
- 1 Oz. horseradish sauce

Recipes

Grill burger patty on gas grill until nearly to desired doneness. Butter and grill bun. Top with 1 slice cooked corned beef and then 1 oz. cheddar cheese. Cover and cook until cheese melts.
Put burger on bun. Serve with chips, 1 oz. horseradish sauce, pickle spear on leaf lettuce.

French Burger

- 1, 5-Oz. burger patty
- ¼ Cup sliced raw mushroom
- 1 small slice red onion
- 1 Oz. blue cheese

Grill burger patty on gas grill until nearly done.
Put sliced mushrooms and cheese on top of burger. Cover and heat for 20-30 seconds. Butter and grill bun. Remove burger from grill and put on bun.

Serve with sliced red onion, pickle on lettuce leaf, choice of potato.

Italian Burger

- 1, 5-Oz. burger patty
- 1 Tbsp. pizza sauce
- 6 slices pepperoni
- 1, 1-Oz. slice mozzarella

Grill burger patty on gas grill until nearly done
Place sauce on burger and top with pepperoni and finally the cheese. Cover and cook until cheese melts. Butter and grill bun. Put burger on bun and serve with choice of potato, pickle on lettuce leaf.

Danish Beef Burger

- 12 Lbs. beef, arm roast
- 3, 12-Oz. beer (Bud)
- 2 Pkg dry onion soup mix
- 1 large yellow onion, chopped

Cut roast into large chunks. Discard excess fat. Place ingredients in large pan. Cook covered for 4-5 hours or until tender. Add water as needed.

Divide beef and au jus into smaller containers to cool. Stir frequently to cool more rapidly. Portion beef and stock into large ziplock bags. Label, date and freeze until needed. Reheat thoroughly before serving.

- 3 Oz. cooked Danish Beer Beef
- 1 Oz. horseradish sauce

Heat ½ Cup or 3 oz. beer beef in microwave. Butter and grill bun. Put hot meat on bun and serve with 1 oz. sauce, pickle on lettuce leaf, choice of potato.

Greek Burger

Marinated Greek Veggies

- 2 Cups chopped onion
- 3 chopped tomatoes
- 1 Cup sliced black olives
- Italian house dressing

Mix veggies together. Pour house dressing over to barely cover. Use 2 Tbsp. on each burger.

- 1, 5-Oz. Burger patty
- 1 whole wheat pita bread
- 2 Tbsp. Greek burger veggie mix
- 1 Oz. Feta cheese

Grill burger on gas grill. Cut 1/3 off top of pita bread. Put veggies inside pita bread. Top with hamburger and then the feta cheese. Serve with potato chips, pickle spear on lettuce leaf.

Mexican Burger

- 1, 5-Oz. Burger patty
- ¼ Cup refried beans
- 1 – 1 Oz. slice Colby
- 1 – 1 Oz. sour cream
- 2 Tbsp. salsa of choice

Grill burger patty until nearly done. Heat refried beans on grill. Top burger with heated refried beans and cheese. Cover until cheese melts. Butter and grill bun. Place burger on bun and serve with salsa and sour cream on the side. Serve with taco chips, pickle on lettuce leaf.

Greek Burger

Marinate equal amounts of black olives - chopped fine, white onions - chopped fine, cherr tom. - halved.

Cover with house dressing

Top with Feta

SALAD

Red Slaw

- 1 red cabbage – shredded
- 2 apples – peeled and sliced
- 10 slices bacon- diced
- 1 onion – diced
- 1 bay leaf
- 1 Cup apple sauce
- 1 Cup cranberry sauce
- 1/3 Cup vinegar
- ½ Cup sugar
- 1 Tsp. chicken soup base

Sauté bacon and onion. Add cabbage, bay leaf, vinegar, and soup base. Cook 20 minutes. Add applesauce and cranberry – mix well. Simmer 5 minutes. Add apples. Mix and serve.

Coleslaw

- 3 Cups mayo
- 2 Cups sugar
- 1 Tsp. black pepper
- 1 Tsp. celery seed
- 1 Tsp. garlic powder
- 2 Tsp. salt
- ½ Cup red wine vinegar
- ½ cub buttermilk
- 4 apples
- 5 Lbs.. slaw mix

Stir all ingredients except apples into a large mixing bowl and stir together until evenly combined. Shred apples using the mandoline and stir into slaw. Store in plastic container, label, date, refrigerate.

Rice Salad

- 6 Cups cooked wild rice
- 1 Cup craisins
- 1 Cup raisins
- 1 Can water chestnuts
- ½ Cup green onions sliced

Garnish with dried salted soy nuts, sliced red onions.

Wild Rice Salad

- 1 Cup wild rice, dry
- 3 Cups water, hot
- 1 Tbsp. oil

Place rice, water and oil in sauce pan. Bring to boil. Cover and reduce heat to a simmer. Cook for 45 minutes or until crunchy/tender, but not mushy. DO NOT OVERCOOK. Drain excess water.

- ¼ Cup oil, salad
- 2 Tbsp. vinegar, wine
- 2 Tsp. soy sauce
- 1 Tsp. sugar
- ¼ Tsp. ground ginger

Combine warm rice with oil, vinegar, soy sauce and spices in a large bowl. Cool, cover, label and refrigerate until needed.

Day of use:

- ¾ Cup bacon, crisp

Fry 1 Lb.. bacon (raw) until crisp or use bacon left-overs from breakfast. Drain well on paper towels.

- 2 tomatoes, ¼ inch diced
- 1 ½ Cups cauliflower, small flowers
- 1 Cup parsley, chopped
- ½ Cup onion, green, ¼ inch diced

Just before serving, fold in bacon, tomatoes,

cauliflower, parsley and onion. Cover, label and refrigerate.

Plate Presentation:

- Spinach lined plate
- 1 ½ Cups wild rice salad
- 3 tomato wedges on top
- 3 Greek olives to garnish

Dressing

- ½ Cup Marukan
- 1 Tbsp. sesame oil
- 1/3 Cup soy sauce
- ½ Tsp. red pepper flakes
- ½ Tsp. black pepper
- 1 Tsp. garlic granulated
- ¼ Tsp. ginger powder

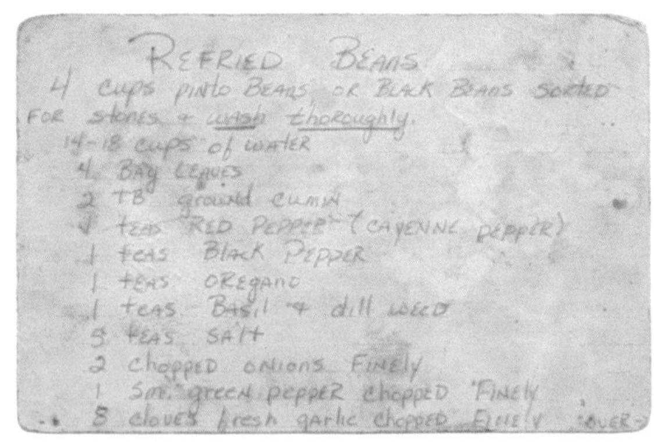

REFRIED BEANS
4 cups pinto Beans or Black Beans sorted for stones + wash thoroughly.
14-18 cups of water
4 Bay Leaves
2 TB ground cumin
1 teas Red Pepper (cayenne pepper)
1 teas Black Pepper
1 teas Oregano
1 teas Basil + dill weed
5 teas salt
2 chopped onions Finely
1 Sm. green pepper chopped Finely
8 cloves fresh garlic chopped Finely -OVER-

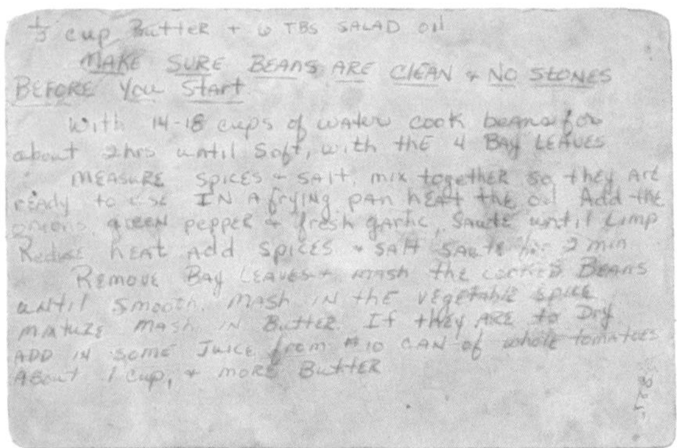

1/2 cup Butter + 6 TBS salad oil
MAKE SURE BEANS ARE CLEAN + NO STONES BEFORE You Start
With 14-18 cups of water cook beans for about 2hrs until Soft, with the 4 Bay Leaves
MEASURE spices + salt, mix together so they are ready to use IN A frying pan heat the oil Add the onions, green pepper + fresh garlic, Saute until Limp
Reduce heat add spices + salt Saute for 2 min
Remove Bay Leaves + mash the cooked Beans until smooth. mash in the vegetable spice mixture mash in Butter. If they are to Dry ADD in some Juice from #10 can of whole tomatoes About 1 cup, + more Butter

Greek Salad

- 2 Cups House (Italian) dressing
- 3 Tbsp. oregano leaf

Combine dressing and oregano. Reserve

- 6 cucumbers, peeled
- 6 tomatoes, ½ inch chunks
- 3 cans garbanzo beans, 15 Oz. each, drained
- 3 Cups olives, black whole
- 2 green peppers, strips
- 1 onion, red, quartered, sliced

Peel cucumbers. Cut in half lengthwise and slice thickly. Combine cucumbers, tomatoes, beans, olives, peppers and onions. Add dressing and mix carefully. Marinate a minimum of 2 hours before serving. Shelf life: 4 days

Plate Presentation:

- Salad bowl lined with lettuce
- 1 ¼ Cup Greek salad on top
- ½ Oz. feta cheese to garnish

SIDES

Refried Beans

- 4 Cups pinto beans or black beans sorted for stones and washed thoroughly.
- 14-18 Cups of water
- 4 bay leaves
- 2 Tbsp. ground cumin
- 1 Tsp. red pepper (cayenne pepper)
- 1 Tsp. black pepper
- 1 Tsp. oregano
- 1 Tsp. basil
- 1 Tsp. dill weed
- 5 Tsp. salt
- 2 finely chopped onions
- 1 small green pepper chopped finely
- 8 cloves fresh garlic chopped finely
- ½ Cup butter and 6 Tbsp. salad oil

MAKE SURE BEANS ARE CLEAN AND NO STONES BEFORE YOU START!

Cook beans in 14-18 cups of water for about 2 hours until soft, with bay leaves. Mix together spices and salt so they are ready to use. In a frying pan heat oil and add onions, green pepper, and fresh garlic. Sauté until limp.

Reduce heat add spices and salt. Sauté for 2 minutes. Remove bay leaves and mash cooked beans until smooth. Mash in the vegetable spice mixture. Mash in butter. If they are too dry add in some juice from a 10 Lbs. can of whole tomatoes. Add about 1 cup and more butter.

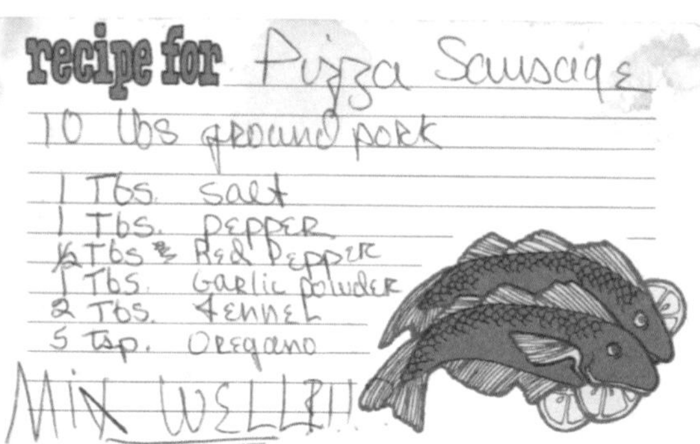

recipe for Pizza Sausage
10 lbs ground pork
1 Tbs. salt
1 Tbs. pepper
½ Tbs = Red Pepper
1 Tbs. Garlic powder
2 Tbs. fennel
5 Tsp. Oregano
MIX WELL!!

SAUSAGES

Pizza Sausage

- 10 Lbs. ground pork
- 1 Tbsp. salt
- 1 Tbsp. pepper
- ½ Tbsp. red pepper
- ½ Tbsp. garlic powder
- 2 Tbsp. fennel
- 5 Tsp. oregano

Mix well! Divide into one pound portions and place in ziplock bags. Label, date and freeze until needed. Thaw and brown off seasoned sausage as needed. Drain off excess fat.

Pizza/Breakfast Sausage

- 10 Lbs pork, ground
- 2 Tbsp. fennel seed
- 1 Tbsp. + 2 Tsp. oregano
- 1 Tbsp. garlic powder
- 1 Tbsp. pepper, black
- 1 Tbsp. salt
- 1 ½ Tsp. pepper, cayenne

Mix pork thoroughly with spices. Portion sausage into 3 Oz. patties. Separate patties with waxed paper. Wrap, label, date and freeze until needed. Thaw and cook to order.

MISC

Beer Batter

- 10 Eggs
- 4 Qts. Red beer
- 1 Tsp. garlic powder
- 1 Tsp. onion powder
- 1 Tsp. paprika
- 2 Tsp. salt
- ½ Tsp. white pepper

Mix in large bowl and add

- 10 Cup flour
- ½ Cup corn starch
- 1 Tsp. baking powder

Caramelized Onions

- 1 Cup sugar
- 1 Cup olive oil
- 1 Tbsp. salt
- 1 Tbsp. pepper
- 1 Tbsp. thyme

Sauté 12 quarts sliced onions until brown. Add 1 Cup red wine. Add 2 Cup red vinegar. Cook down to reduce liquid.

Marinated Vegetables

- 8 carrots, peeled
- 4 heads broccoli, trimmed
- 2 heads cauliflower, trimmed

Clean and trim vegetables. Cut into bite-sized pieces.

- 2 cans water chestnuts, 4 Oz each drained

Combine vegetables and water chestnuts in large container. Mix well.

- 1 Qt. House dressing

Pour dressing over vegetables. Toss. Cover, and refrigerate until used. Marinate a minimum of 2 hours before serving. Shelf life: 4 days

BREADS

French Bread

- 3 qt warm water
- 1/3 Cup yeast
- 1/3 Cup salt
- 8 Qts. bread flour

Blend yeast and water in mixer on speed 2 for 5 minutes, using dough hook. Start adding bread flour gradually while still mixing. When 4 scoops of bread flour have been added, add the salt. Add remaining bread flour. When mixture has become dough, increases to speed 3 and mix for 7-10 minutes. Remove from mixer and knead on floured surface. Proof until almost doubled in size then score loaves. Bake in combination oven at 375 for 10 minutes. Reduce heat to 250-300 and bake for an additional 15-20 minutes.

Walnut-Pepper Biscotti
3½ dozen (con ½ recipe)

3½ c — 1¾ c flour
1 t — ½ t. baking soda
1 t — ½ t " powder
¼ t — ⅛ t. salt
(sift into bowl, mix in pepper)
1 T. — 1½ t fresh gr. black pepper
1 c — ½ c unsalt. butter, rm temp.
2 c — 1 c sugar
(beat butter cream in sugar - lgt & fluffy)
4 — 2 lg eggs, rm. temp (one at a time)
4 t. — 2 t grated orange peel
1 T. — 1½ t vanilla
½ t. — ¼ t almond extract
(mix in)
3 c — 1½ c walnuts, lghtly toasted coarsely chop (app. 6oz) 12oz (mix in)

add dry ingred til just blened - cover w/ suran - chill til hard — overnight (one day ahead)
oven 350° - flour & butter 2 baking sheets
roll dough into 3 logs 1½" wide
Bake 2 on 1 sheet, one on other - 20 mins
light brown - cool slightly (5-10 mins)
Cut diagonally crosswise ¾" wide
Lay down on sheets & bake 15 mins
more til golden - cool on racks
store air tight

Correction: 1 Tbsp. + 1 Tsp. grated orange people

Wild Rice Nut Bread

- 4 Cups all purpose flour
- 2/3 Cup sugar
- 1 Tsp. salt
- 2 Tbsp. baking powder
- 2 Cup milk
- 3 eggs
- 2/3 Cup oil
- 4 Cup walnuts chopped
- 1 Cup wild rice, cooked
- 1 Cup dried cherries/raisins

Sift together all dry ingredients. Mix milk, eggs

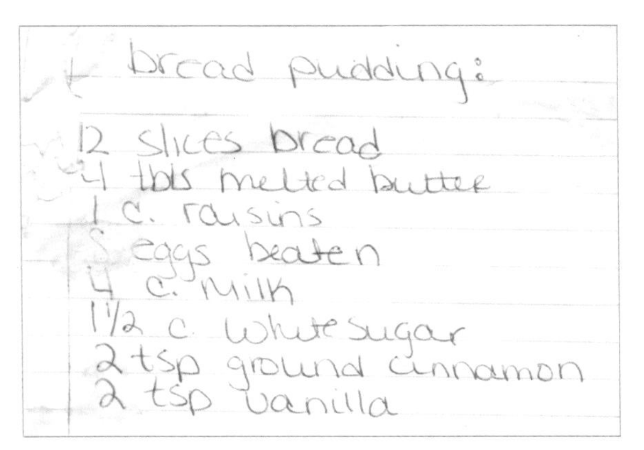

bread pudding:

12 slices bread
4 tbls melted butter
1 c. raisins
5 eggs beaten
4 c. milk
1½ c white sugar
2 tsp ground cinnamon
2 tsp vanilla

and oil. Add wet ingredients to dry ingredients, careful not to over mix. Fold in walnuts and wild rice. Portion into loaf pans (flexi pans, sprayed). Bake at 325-350 for 20-30 minutes.

ICE CREAM AND SORBETS

Ice Cream Base

- 3 qt half and half
- 1 Tsp. vanilla
- 30 egg yolks
- 1 Lb. + 6 Oz. sugar

Mix yolks and half of sugar in mixer. Combine other half of sugar with half and half and vanilla in double boiler and heat to 185. Temper yolk mixture then combine with cream and continue to cook until mixture coats back of wooden spoon. Strain and cool in an ice bath.

Coffee Ice Cream

- 3 ½ Cups cream
- 2 ½ Cups whole milk
- 6 egg yolks
- 1 Cup sugar
- 1 Tsp. vanilla
- ¼ Cup coffee
- 1 Oz.. Kahlua

Lemon Ice Cream

- 4 eggs
- 1 Cup lemon juice (fresh squeezed)
- 1 Cup sugar
- 2 Tsp. lemon extract
- 3 Cups heavy cream
- 1 Cup whole milk

Mix eggs, sugar and juice in stainless pan and cook over low heat till it thickens. Off heat, whip in the cream, milk and extract.

Strain and freeze in ice cream maker.

Rick Chocolate Ice Cream

- 4 Cups heavy cream
- 2 Cups whole milk
- 4 Oz. Hersheys cocoa
- 1 Cup sugar
- 1 Tbsp. vanilla
- 1 Cup strong coffee
- ¼ Cup Folgers granulated coffee
- 1 Lb. semi sweet chocolate

Whip together:
- 10 egg yolks
- 1 Cup sugar

Put 1 Cup cream and cocoa in pan, simmer 5 minutes till cocoa is thoroughly cooked.
Add rest of cream, milk and 1 Cup sugar bring to about 180 degrees. Put both coffees and semi-sweet chocolate in large bowl. Temper egg mix, then add to cream mixture in pan.

Cook at 180 degrees for a time. Cool in water bath and add vanilla. Strain through a fine chinois. Freeze in ice cream machine.

Lemon Meringue Pie (10 inch pie)

2 c. sugar
½ c. cornstarch
2 c. water
4 egg yolks - slightly beaten
2 drops yellow food coloring
¼ c. butter or oleo
2 t. grated lemon peel
⅔ c. lemon juice

Bake pie shell. Heat oven to 400°. Mix sugar + cornstarch in medium saucepan. Gradually stir in water. Cook over medium heat, stirring constantly until mixture thickens + boils. Boil + stir 1 minute. Gradually stir at least half the hot mixture in egg yolks. Blend into hot mixture in pan. Boil + stir 2 min (1 min for 9" pie) Remove from heat; stir in butter, lemon peel, lemon juice + food color. Pour into baked pie shell.

Heap meringue onto hot pie filling - spread over filling, carefully sealing meringue to edge of crust to prevent shrinking or weeping.
Bake about 10 min or until a delicate brown
Cool away from draft.

9 inch pie
1½ c. sugar
⅓ c. plus 1 T. cornstarch
1½ c. water
3 egg yolks - slightly beaten
3 T. butter or oleo
2 t. grated lemon peel
½ c. lemon juice
2 drops yellow food coloring

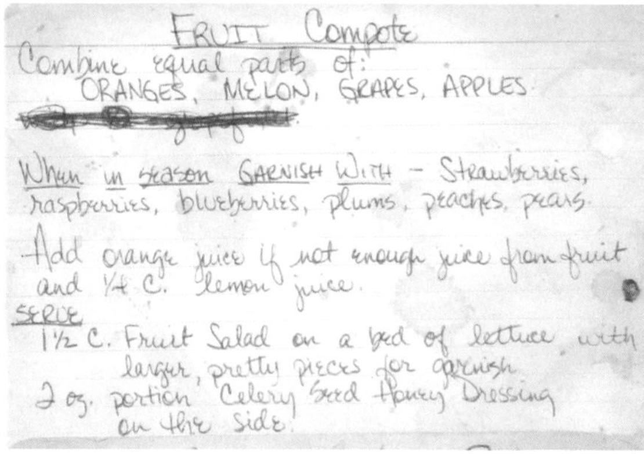

FRUIT Compote

Combine equal parts of:
ORANGES, MELON, GRAPES, APPLES

When in season GARNISH WITH - Strawberries, raspberries, blueberries, plums, peaches, pears.

Add orange juice if not enough juice from fruit and ¼ C. lemon juice.

SERVE
1½ C. Fruit Salad on a bed of lettuce with larger, pretty pieces for garnish
2 oz. portion Celery Seed Honey Dressing on the side.

Sorbets with Simple Syrup Base

Simple Syrup Base

- 1 Pt. water
- 1 Lb. sugar
- 1 Tbsp. lemon juice

Mix together and cook over high heat until boiling. Stir to dissolve sugar and cool.

Lemon or Lime

- Base plus 12 Oz. lemon or lime juice and 1 Pt. water

Orange or Mango

- Base plus 4 Pt.s. blend fruit juice

Raspberry/Strawberry/Kiwi/Melon

- Base plus 2 Lbs. + 4 Oz. strained fruit puree, 2 Oz. lemon juice, and 8 Oz. water

Pineapple

- 2/3 Cup simple syrup, 3 ½ Cup pureed fruit, and ¼ Cup water

Cantaloupe

- 2/3 Cup simple syrup, 1 large cantaloupe, pureed, ¼ Cup water, and 1 Tbsp. port wine

Apple Cider Sorbet

- 4.5 Oz. sugar
- 4 Oz. water
- 7 Oz. apples, peeled/cored/chopped
- 5.5 Oz. cider, and 1 Tsp. spices

Heat water and sugar in pan until sugar dissolves. Add apples and cook until tender. Add cider and simmer. Puree in blender until very smooth. Strain and chill.

Peppered Raspberry Sorbet

- 4 Cups raspberries
- 4 1 Cup sugar

Peppered Raspberry Sorbet

- 4 cups Raspberries
- 1 cup Sugar
- 1 cup orange juice
- 2 oz. lemon juice
- 2 oz Chambord
- 1 tsp fresh ground black pepper
- 1/8 tsp cayanne pepper

- 4 1 Cup orange juice
- 4 2 Oz. lemon juice
- 4 2 Oz. Chambord
- 4 1 Tsp. fresh ground black pepper
- 1/8 Tsp. cayenne pepper

Chocolate Sorbet

- 2 Cup water
- ¼ Cup cocoa powder
- ½ Cup sugar
- 4 Oz. chocolate chips
- 1 Tbsp. corn syrup
- 1 Cup orange juice

Bring water, cocoa, sugar to boil. Pour mixture over chocolate chips. Stir until well combined. Add corn syrup and orange juice. Chill mixture.

DESSERTS

Flourless Chocolate Torte

Preheat oven to 375 and butter 2, 10-inch round baking pans. Line bottom with a round of wax paper and butter paper.

- 2 Lbs. bittersweet chocolate chopped into small pieces
- 1 Lb. butter
- 12 eggs room temperature

Place chocolate and butter in a double boiler or metal bowl set over a saucepan of barely simmering water. Melt chocolate with butter; stir until smooth. Mix eggs with whip in mixer for 8 minutes. Whip into chocolate and butter mixture until well combined. Portion into pans. Make sure to use water bath. Bake 35 minutes. Check after 20 minutes and 5 minute intervals until done.

Chocolate Bread Pudding

- 10 slices cubed bread
- 3 Cups Half & Half
- 1 Cup heavy cream
- 3 eggs, whole
- 8 egg yolks
- ½ Cup sugar
- 1 Tsp. vanilla
- 8 Oz.. white chocolate

Melt chocolate in a double boiler. In a saucepan, heat Half & Half and heavy cream to scalding point. In bowl, beat eggs and yolks and sugar until well blended. Whisk in some of the hot cream mixture to temper egg mixture. Whisk in remaining hot cream mixture, chocolate and vanilla. Pour over bread. Bake at 350, 40-50 minutes in 13 x 9 x 2" baking dish until knife inserted comes out clean. 10 servings. Serve with vanilla sauce.

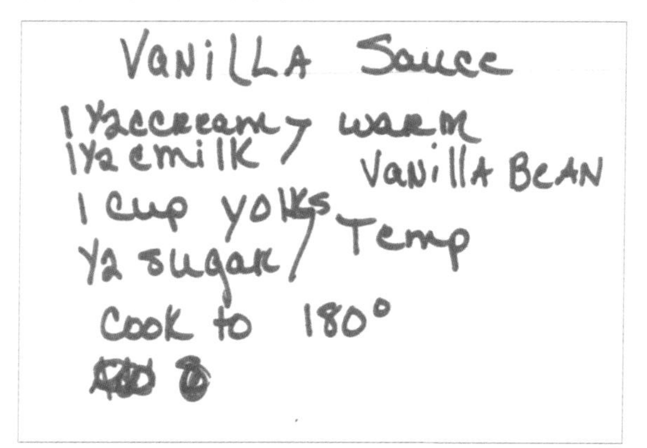

VANILLA Sauce

1 ½ c cream } warm
1 ½ c milk
Vanilla BEAN
1 cup yolks } Temp
½ sugar
Cook to 180°

Chocolate Molten Cake Batter

- 2 Lbs. cubed butter
- 2 Lbs. semi-sweet chocolate, chopped
- 16 eggs
- 16 yolks
- 2 Cups sugar
- 2 Tbsp. + 2 Tsp. flour

Melt chocolate and butter together over double boiler. Mix eggs and sugar on high speed until light colored, thick and frothy. Add egg mixture to chocolate mixture and quickly fold in flour, careful not to over mix. Divide into containers and refrigerate for at least 2 hours before use.

Crème Brulée

- 24 egg yolks
- 3 Qts. heavy cream
- 12 Oz. sugar
- 2 whole vanilla beans

Split vanilla beans and scrape out seeds. Add seeds and bean with heavy cream in a stainless pan. (not aluminum) Scald the cream; do not boil it. Whip yolks with sugar until combined and pour scalded cream into the eggs in a thin stream until combined. Strain with mesh strainer, skim off foam. Place ramekins on full sheet tray and fill each to the top, place sheet tray in oven. Add hot water to come up almost to the top of ramekins. Bake at 325 for 45 minutes until custard sets. Cool, wrap on half sheet trays.

The Lake Superior Margarita is by far my fondest Maggie's drink. Every spring I would meet friends for a margarita!

—Ruth Goetz

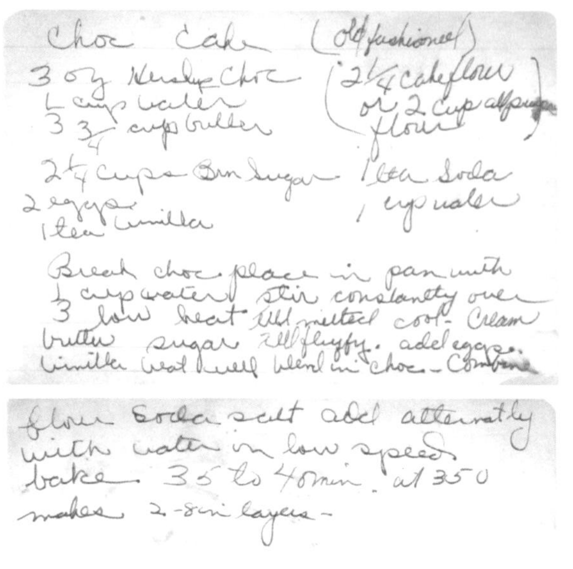

Choc Cake (old fashioned)

3 oz Hershey Choc
1/2 cup water
3/4 cup butter
2 1/4 cups Brn sugar
2 eggs
1 tea vanilla

(2 1/4 cake flour or 2 cup all purpose flour)
1 tea soda
1 cup water

Break choc. place in pan with 1/3 cup water stir constantly over low heat till melted cool. Cream butter sugar till fluffy. add eggs. vanilla beat well blend in choc. Combine flour soda salt add alternatly with water on low speed. bake 35 to 40 min. at 350 makes 2-8 in layers.

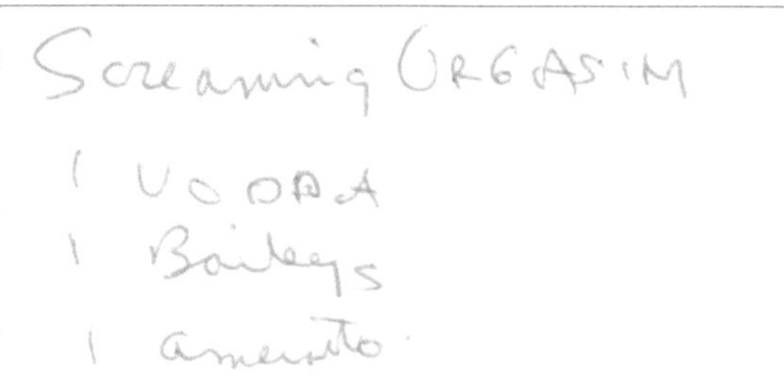

Screaming ORGASIM

1 Vodka
1 Baileys
1 amaretto

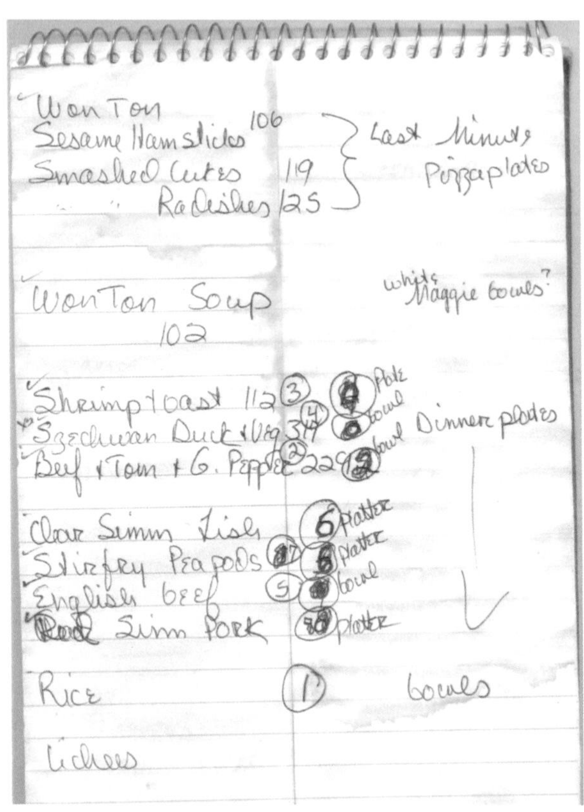

Won Ton
Sesame Ham sticks 106
Smashed Cukes 119
Radishes 125
} Last Minute
Pizza plates

Won Ton Soup
102

white Maggie bowls?

Shrimp toast 112 (3) plate
Szechwan Duck + Veg 314 (4) bowl
Beef + Tom + G. Pepper (2) 229 bowl
Dinner plates

Clear Simm Fish (6) platter
Stirfry Peapods (6) platter
English beef (5) bowl
Red Simm Pork platter

Rice (1) bowls

Lichees

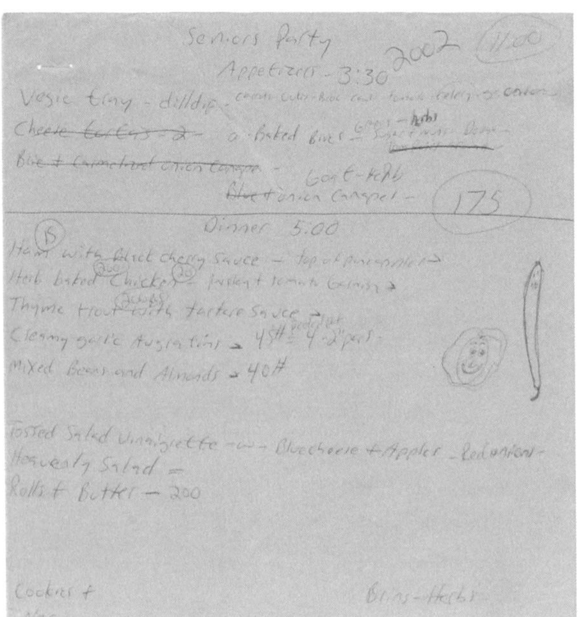

Seniors Party 2002 (1100)

Appetizers - 3:30

Vegie tray - dilldip - [illegible]

~~Cheese [illegible]~~ - Baked Brie [illegible]

~~Brie + Carmelized onion Canape~~ - Goat - Herb ~~Blue~~ + onion Canapé - (175)

Dinner 5:00

(15) Ham with Black cherry Sauce - top of pineapple [illegible]

Herb baked Chicken - parsley + tomato [illegible]

Thyme trout with tartere Sauce

Creamy garlic Augratins - 45# - 4-2" pans

Mixed Beans and Almonds - 40#

Tossed Salad Vinaigrette - w - Bluecheese + Apples - Red onions -

Heavenly Salad -

Rolls + Butter - 200

Cookies +

Brins - Herbs

The people make it happen

Above: Sandy Pavola. Below: Marie Nelson

Left: Mike and Sharon Bonney. Left middle: Mark Simmons, Dawn Hauser, Kevin Karaba. Left bottom: Steve Soderman, Morris Boutin

Above, Robert Parsonage, Janet Sternat

Below: Jane Sherman, Steve Soderman

Paraphernalia
Memorabilia
Ka - Ka
Stuff

MHR Original Flamingo T - Shirts ^^^^^^^^^^^^-10.50
Maggie's Beer List T - Shirts^^^^^^^^^^^^^^^^^-14.00
I Love Maggie's Beer Long Sleeve^^^^^^^^^^^^^-26.00
Maggie' Sweat Shirts ^^^^^^^^^^^^^^^^^^-21.00
Maggie's Watches ^^^^^^^^^^^^^^^^^^^^^^-26.25
Maggie's Beer Cooler ^^^^^^^^^^^^^^^^^^^^^-4.25
Maggie's Hats ^^^^^^^^^^^^^^^^^^^^^^^^^^-8.00
Maggie's Aprons ^^^^^^^^^^^^^^^^^^^^^^^^-10.50
Maggie's Sun Visors ^^^^^^^^^^^^^^^^^^^^^^-3.25

We guarantee that you will look absolutely marvelous in any of our Maggie's Stuff even if your mother dressed you funny as a kid!!

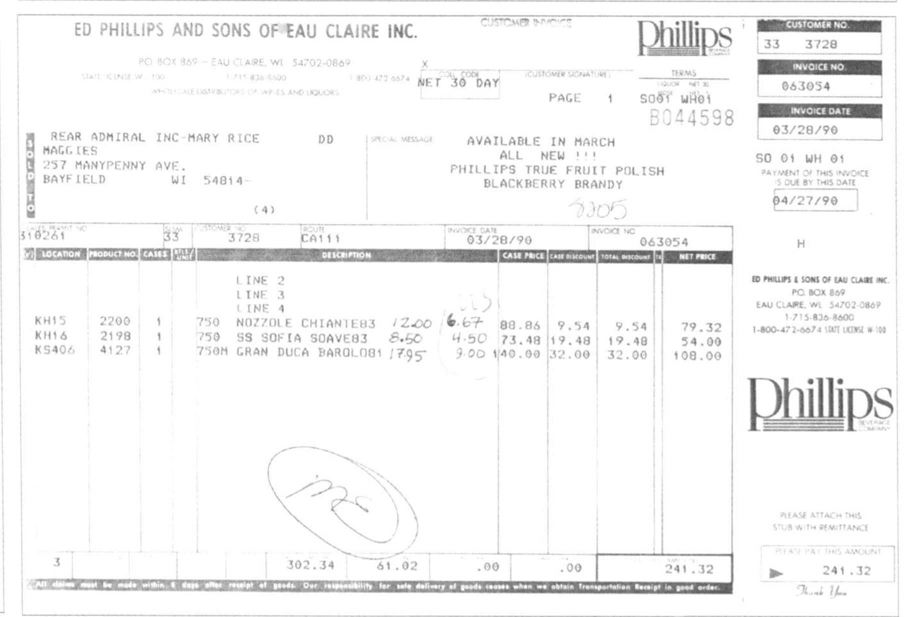

ED PHILLIPS AND SONS OF EAU CLAIRE INC.

CUSTOMER INVOICE

Phillips

P.O. BOX 869 — EAU CLAIRE, WI 54702-0869

STATE LICENSE W-100 1-715-836-8600 1-800-472-6674

WHOLESALE DISTRIBUTORS OF WINES AND LIQUORS

COLL CODE: NET 30 DAY

X (CUSTOMER SIGNATURE)

TERMS

PAGE 1 SO01 WH01

B044598

SOLD TO:
REAR ADMIRAL INC-MARY RICE DD
MAGGIES
257 MANYPENNY AVE.
BAYFIELD WI 54814-
(4)

SPECIAL MESSAGE:
AVAILABLE IN MARCH
ALL NEW !!!
PHILLIPS TRUE FRUIT POLISH
BLACKBERRY BRANDY

SALES PERMIT NO	SLSM	CUSTOMER NO	ROUTE	INVOICE DATE	INVOICE NO
310261	33	3728	CA111	03/28/90	063054

LOCATION	PRODUCT NO.	CASES	BTLS/UNIT	DESCRIPTION	CASE PRICE	CASE DISCOUNT	TOTAL DISCOUNT	TX	NET PRICE
				LINE 2					
				LINE 3					
				LINE 4					
KH15	2200	1		750 NOZZOLE CHIANTE83	88.86	9.54	9.54		79.32
KH16	2198	1		750 SS SOFIA SOAVE83	73.48	19.48	19.48		54.00
KS406	4127	1		750M GRAN DUCA BAROLO81	140.00	32.00	32.00		108.00
3				302.34	61.02	.00	.00		241.32

All claims must be made within 5 days after receipt of goods. Our responsibility for safe delivery of goods ceases when we obtain Transportation Receipt in good order.

CUSTOMER NO.: 33 3728

INVOICE NO.: 063054

INVOICE DATE: 03/28/90

SO 01 WH 01

PAYMENT OF THIS INVOICE IS DUE BY THIS DATE: 04/27/90

H

ED PHILLIPS & SONS OF EAU CLAIRE INC.
P.O. BOX 869
EAU CLAIRE, WI. 54702-0869
1-715-836-8600
1-800-472-6674 STATE LICENSE W-100

Phillips BEVERAGE COMPANY

PLEASE ATTACH THIS STUB WITH REMITTANCE

PLEASE PAY THIS AMOUNT ▶ 241.32

Thank You

Working at Maggie's

Above: Liz Boyd
Below: Lucas DePerry

Above: Karmyn Simmons
Below: Elizabeth Simmons

Top, front to back: Katie Poch, Matt Gordon, Drayk Hoopman. Above: Chris Hillert, Karmyn Simmons. Bottom, l-r: Larry Soulier, Lisa Bresette (on floor) and Karmyn Simmons

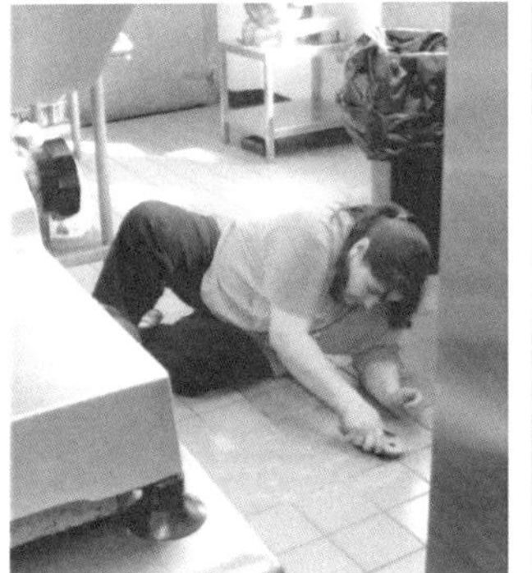

And The Walls Came Down
2020

MO HOTTA-MO BETTA
Peace

Accolades and goodbyes

JUST ONE-OF-A-KIND

The town is losing a passionate voice for the community, and for food. Mary always had great, unique ideas, and she was just full of fun. The "Flamingos Up North" theme boils down to FUN. She named the corporation after it and she's certainly provided that to the community.

After stepping away from Wild Rice in 2017 and stepping down from Northland College's Board of Trustees in 2019, Rice put the finishing touch on her career. "With in-restaurant dining shut down because of the pandemic, neither Rice nor the community can appropriately celebrate the end of an era," Nelson said. "But I think we're all grateful that we've had Mary in our lives. The restaurants are a small part of her largess with her support of Big Top Chautauqua and Northland College. The list goes on and on. She was just one-of-a-kind."

—*Heidi Nelson*

AWARD FOR VOLUNTEERISM

A driving force in the nonprofit community for decades, Mary H. Rice received the 2019 Jerry & Mary Phillips Bayfield Award for Volunteerism, presented at the Bayfield Heritage Association. Her leadership, vision, and involvement in local organizations helped shape the Bayfield community's quality of life. Many people expressed gratitude for all she has done in our little town.

—*Wendy Cariveau*

Above: Beth Meyers, Jerry Phillips, Mary Rice
Below: Molly Rice and Mary

GOVERNOR'S ARTS AWARDS GIVEN

Two people and two organizations received a Governor's Awards in Support of the Arts for 1998, the 18th year for the awards. One of the recipients was Mary Hulings Rice—painter, singer, and performer—whose patronage and vigorous hands-on involvement "has energized the arts of northern Wisconsin" according to the Wisconsin Foundation for the Arts, a non-profit group that sponsors the awards.

Mary Rice was recognized for her patronage and hands-on involvement in the arts in northern Wisconsin. Rice has subsidized annual concerts by the St. Paul Orchestra at Northland College, helped start Lake Superior Big Top Chautauqua and the Madeline Island Music Camp, and is credited with bringing HRK Foundation support to Ashland and Bayfield Counties.

MARY RICE AND BIGTOP

My memories of Mary Rice begin with founding Lake Superior Big Top Chautauqua. She let us lease her property at Mount Ashwabay for $1 and her family's MAHADH Foundation provided financing for our expenses. Until we received our non-profit status, I was required to send them a copy of every check I wrote. We had no office or copy machine, so for that first summer of 1986 I alternated between Tom Lindsey's law office, Bremer Bank and the Bayfield Chamber of Commerce, asking them to make the copies.

For the first year or so, we met regularly with Mary so that she could be involved with all our plans. She was always enthusiastic and supportive. Cast parties at Mary's were both fun and times to reflect and realize that the hard work was well worth the product.

Maggie's was such a wonderful, happy place to meet friends and discuss the problems of the world, celebrate a special time, or gather to plan before a meeting and always the flamingos! I will never see a flamingo without thinking fondly of Mary. I have been to the flamingo sanctuary in Great Inagua, Bahamas where there are at least 50,000 of those magnificent birds but I always think of the Maggie's décor.

—Carolyn Sneed

Mary's car moves to a new home on the Island in the care of Tommy Nelson. Photo: Kye M. Castillo

MARY RICE: BORN JULY 22, 1940

On December 2, 2020, Mary Hulings Rice, age 80, of Bayfield, passed away at her residence. She was born Mary Elizabeth Hulings in Stillwater, the daughter of Bill and Betty (Andersen) Hulings.

Mary attended Stillwater High School and graduated from Carleton College (Northfield, MN). While at Carleton, she met John Rice and they were married in 1963. She worked as a secretary in Minneapolis until John, who was an officer in the US Army, was sent to Germany. She and John lived in Baumholder, Germany from 1967-69, where their first child, Molly, was born, and then Warrington, England from 1969-70, where Katherine was born. Mary and John returned to live in St. Paul, MN in 1970 until they were divorced in 1979. Divorce was a relative term to Mary, and she considered John, his wife Barbara, and their daughter, immediate family.

In 1973, with sister Martha Kaemmer and friend Steve Soderman, Mary opened Thrice, a cookware store on Grand Avenue in St. Paul, which soon took over the neighboring storefront and became a cooking school. She and friend Carole Howe, a fellow Grand Avenue business owner, created the yearly celebration known as Grand Old Day.

Mary moved to Bayfield, WI in 1980. She had traveled there for summers since she was a child when her father purchased the Shaw farm on Sand Island. **Mary opened Maggie's in 1980, where pink flamingos became the identifiable symbol. Maggie's closed December 31, 2020. Mary's other restaurants and food-related businesses over the years in Bayfield included Mainstreet Maggie's, Bates Bar, and The Egg Toss.**

In 1983, Mary purchased The Clubhouse restaurant on Madeline Island, which became well renowned in foodie communities. She closed The Clubhouse in 1999 to open an adored eating experience, Wild Rice Restaurant, in the woods on the shore of Lake Superior south of Bayfield. Wild Rice closed in 2017, but the experience she began lives on in the form of a retreat center.

She had a hand in starting so many other businesses: Big Top Chautauqua, Madeline Island Music Camp, CORE Community Resources, to name a few. And she served on the boards of Northland College and the Madeline Island Ferry Line. She also encouraged development of nonprofits such as Apostle Islands Historic Preservation Conservation and Apostle Islands Area Community Fund.

The "Queen of Bayfield", Mary was an impresario extraordinaire who organized countless dinners, parties, events, mystery tours and celebrations. **She founded the Blue Moon Ball, Northern New Years, the Fun Hogs, the Rump Committee and F.U.N. (Flamingos Up North), the umbrella for her many restaurants.**

She led tours for family and friends to exotic places, art museums, vineyards and fine restaurants around the world as well as to her beloved Rasina in Umbria, Italy, and Hope Town, Bahamas, where she became a central figure in the community. Each trip was planned down to the last detail to make sure all could experience it fully.

In Bayfield, her home was open to everyone—no knocking on the door, just walk in—everyone, that is, except tourists who thought her Queen Anne house was a B&B. She held court from her chair in the solarium, where she would be planning the next occasion to gather friends together.

Mary touched many lives with her unlimited generosity while demanding excellence from organizations and people she supported. She was discerning and strategic in her philanthropy yet immediately responded to emergency needs, no matter the cause. Her giving wasn't encumbered by ego; she truly seemed fine with providing people a place to start and then letting them run with it.

Though she was often a "larger than life" character, Mary was also a gifted artist—watercolors her specialty—and a singer in choirs and at Sunday Church on Sand Island. She had a gift for storytelling and story-making experiences were guaranteed with Mary. While she loved the notoriety that came with being the "Queen", she also felt a deep responsibility for Bayfield and its welfare.

She loved to read, a book a night sometimes. Her vocabulary was vast and vulgar. She had wit that didn't quit, and creativity without limit. She was a list maker and a problem solver.

Mary is survived by her two daughters, Mary "Molly" Rice (Dan Priebe) of Hudson, WI, and Katherine (Rice) Hayes of St. Paul, MN; a "bonus daughter" Alison (Cody) Urhammer of Hudson, WI; and four grandchildren: Sam Priebe, Zeno Priebe, Sevona Hayes, and Tysen Hayes, and last but not least, her "right hand" life and project manager, Margaret Erickson of Bayfield, WI.

She was preceded in death by her parents; a sister, Martha Kaemmer; a best friend, Karlyn Holman; and three Sand Island soul mates, Warren, Peter, and Tom Jensch.

MARY—A WONDERFUL LADY

Bayfield would not be the town it is without her. She was the Queen of Bayfield.

One day I was watering plants on the deck of the Chart House at Superior Rentals. Six ladies were having coffee and one of them said, "She must own this place too." I asked who they were referring to and they said, "Mary Rice." I smiled. "No, she doesn't. I do." Their response was, "Then you must be Little Mary Rice." I thanked them.

Mary was my idol. We will miss her. She was kind beyond words.

—Susan K. Defoe, born and raised in Bayfield

WILL NOT BE THE SAME

Bayfield will not be the same without Mary. My grandparents, Bertram and Birgit Noreng, were nearby so we heard wonderful stories about her. One trip to Maggie's made it our favorite lunch place when visiting Bayfield and she hosted us once in her lovely home. Mary treated us like family. RIP Queen Mary. You will be missed.

—Linda and Don Shearer

Phil Anich and Mary

A toast to you, Mary

When guests left Sand Island and turned to wave goodbye, Mary loved to "give them a moon" from the dock. So, it was only fair that, for her 60th birthday, she received a MASS MOON from friends.

Above: Mary and Junior Yeska. Below: Becky Lind and Mary
Above right: Mary in "the tub" with Martha, Mary's sister, ready to assist.

October 20, 2020

Dear Friends of Maggie's

Moving through these uncertain times and with the daily changing industry landscapes, on December 31st, 2020, the doors to Maggie's will be closing permanently and I will be retiring from the restaurant world.

Maggie's was my first and will likely be my last foray in the wild, wacky, and crazy life profession of restaurateur. Over these many decades my pursuit for quality, unique, and delightfully fun dining brought Main Street Maggie's, The Clubhouse on Madeline Island, The Cheeseboard, Two Girls Catering, The Egg Toss Bakery Café and Wild Rice Restaurant, to the Chequamegon Bay. I will always cherish the memories I have made with each of you over the years as you supported my dreams. I have been blessed with hundreds of excellent and faithful employees and thousands of the most incredible customers. Please accept my deepest thanks for your service and your loyalty to all my restaurants. I would love to have a farewell event to honor you and my employees, but due to the current restrictions, at this time I am unable to do so.

Finally, It is with extreme gratitude and appreciation that Maggie's has been able to serve this community for the last 40 years and I thank you all for an amazing life.

The Queen

Mary

CPSIA information can be obtained
at www.ICGtesting.com
Printed in the USA
LVRC101224161121
703473LV00003B/129

* 9 7 8 0 9 9 6 8 0 7 1 8 0 *